GOD, MAN AND HISTORY

Contemporary Jewish Thought
from Shalem Press:

Essential Essays on Judaism
Eliezer Berkovits

*The Dawn: Political Teachings
of the Book of Esther*
Yoram Hazony

GOD, MAN
AND HISTORY

ELIEZER BERKOVITS

Edited by David Hazony

SHALEM PRESS
JERUSALEM

First edition 1959. Second edition 1965.
Third edition 1979. Fourth edition 2004.

Fourth Printing, 2014

Cover design: Erica Halivni
Cover picture: "Lower Slopes of Mount Sinai" (1839)
Copyright © Historical Picture Archive/Corbis

Distribution:
Shalem Press, 3 Ha'askan Street
Jerusalem 9378010, Israel
Tel.: (02) 560-5577

E-mail: shalemorder@shalem.ac.il
www.shalem.ac.il
ISBN 978-965-7052-15-0

Printed in Israel

CONTENTS

Foreword

In the three decades prior to the rise of Nazism, Germany gave birth to a generation of Jewish thinkers without precedent in recent centuries. Luminaries whose work can be associated with the ferment in Berlin and Frankfurt during this period include Hermann Cohen, Franz Rosenzweig, Martin Buber, Abraham Joshua Heschel, Emil Fackenheim, Menachem Mendel Schneerson, Yehiel Jacob Weinberg, and Joseph B. Soloveitchik. In recent years, it has become increasingly evident that one of the most creative figures within this elite group was Eliezer Berkovits (1908-1992), whose 19 books and hundreds of essays and articles broke new ground in nearly every area of Jewish thought, including theology, philosophy of law, Bible studies, the meaning of Jewish history, nationalism and Zionism, and contemporary trends in Jewish and Western thought.

Despite the breadth and depth of his writings, Berkovits did not attain during his lifetime the level of recognition enjoyed by other major Jewish thinkers. This, for a number of reasons: In part because he did not have the same tools for the promulgation of his work, such as the support of a major university or publishing house; in part because he spent his most productive years in Chicago, far from the center of Jewish intellectual life in America; and in part because his writing did not conform to the styles and schools that were fashionable in philosophy in his

day. Yet he maintained a dedicated following of scholars, rabbis, and laymen of all denominations, and recent years have
seen a significant revival of interest in his works. Among the
signs of renewed interest have been the publication of a collec-
tion of his essays, *Essential Essays on Judaism* (2002), and the
establishment of the Eliezer Berkovits Institute for Jewish
Thought at the Shalem Center, based in Jerusalem. One of the
Institute's central projects is the re-publication of all of Berkovits'
major works, many of which have been out of print for a
generation, as well as their translation from English into
Hebrew.

This edition of *God, Man and History* marks the inaugural
volume of this series. The decision to publish this work first
reflects its significance within the corpus of Berkovits' writings,
as it is properly viewed as the keystone. First published in 1959,
it examines the underpinnings of Judaism as a whole, from
theology to law to the meaning of Jewish nationhood. In contrast to other twentieth-century thinkers, who employed the
classic Jewish sources to defend a modernist outlook, or who
wrote meditations on the Jewish experience in the style of
contemporary philosophical trends, Berkovits' work offers an
argument for the independence and validity of a traditional
Jewish worldview in a manner reminiscent of Judah Halevi,
Maimonides, and Saadia Gaon. *God, Man and History* is attuned
to developments in modern thought, offering not only an exploration of the foundations of Judaism, but also their presentation as a coherent approach that may be contrasted with the
central streams of Western philosophy since Hume and Kant.

The rationalist expository method that Berkovits adopted
has obvious limitations. Based in argument rather than in exis-
tentialist description, it yields a work that is more challenging to
read, and more vulnerable to criticism, than much of recent
Jewish thought. But this sort of clear, methodical approach was,
in Berkovits' view, a pressing need for Judaism, which he

believed to have been in a state of intellectual crisis since the advent of modern philosophy—a crisis that had led the majority of Jews to despair of their religion in its traditional form, and to abandon it in favor of either a thoroughgoing secularism or a Judaism reconstituted under fundamentally new premises.

The central weakness of modern Western thought, Berkovits argued, is not its rejection of religion but its inability to provide a compelling basis for moral action. The modern era in philosophy is often said to have begun with Descartes' "I think, therefore I am," a descriptive statement from which all understanding is assumed to follow by means of the strict application of reason. But as modern philosophers quickly learned, this method, in both its deductive and empirical versions, runs aground precisely where it tries to move from the strictly descriptive to the prescriptive—that is, from "is" to "ought."

This difficulty was first articulated in full form in the thought of David Hume (who was the subject of Berkovits' doctoral dissertation), but was also confronted, in a different context, by Immanuel Kant, whose writings form the basis of much of modern ethics. Kant sought to build an approach to morality based purely on rational statements. He was forced to concede, however, that while such a method may describe ethical action in theory, it cannot explain why anyone should decide to act on the basis of this theory. In his *Grounding for the Metaphysics of Morals*, Kant acknowledged: "But how pure reason can be practical by itself without other incentives taken from whatever source... to explain this is quite beyond the power of human reason, and all the effort and work of seeking such an explanation is wasted."*

To Berkovits, this difficulty has had far-reaching consequences for the modern age, the most important of which is the inability

---

* Immanuel Kant, *Grounding for the Metaphysics of Morals*, trans. James W. Ellington (Indianapolis: Hackett, 1981), p. 60.

to maintain a consistent, effective dedication to moral behavior. According to Berkovits, it is perhaps the central incongruity of Western civilization that despite steady progress in science and technology—that is, in the rationalization of nature and its utilization for human ends—modern man is nonetheless unable to advance on the ethical plane. Indeed, he has undertaken the most ambitious acts of barbarism the world has known, of which twentieth-century Nazism and Communism are only the most extreme cases. "The evil done by the power that knowledge provides," he writes, "has always eclipsed the good done by the same power. Notwithstanding enlightenment, man seems to remain an essentially unethical being." (p. 100)

As opposed to modern philosophy, Judaism starts with a different first principle, which does not merely describe existence, but also asserts the presence of a moral will and a binding moral ideal. It therefore incorporates not only the descriptive but also the prescriptive realm. "The foundation of religion," Berkovits writes, "is not the affirmation that God *is*, but that God is concerned with man and the world; that, having created this world, he has not abandoned it, leaving it to its own devices; that he cares about his creation." (p. 15)

What we know about God, explains Berkovits, we know not from speculation but from experience, of which the prophetic encounter is the central, foundational example, and from our memory of that experience as passed on in tradition. It is the encounter alone that provides us with our "raw data," and from there we know that revelation is not simply a matter of factual, but also of moral, truth. Judaism does not require the fabrication of "other incentives taken from whatever source" to induce moral behavior; rather, such behavior follows from the concern for the world which God has revealed, the major implication of which is that man, too, must be concerned with human history and progress. This is the central content of the revelation on which religion is based; without it, morality is forever undermined.

This central thesis—that God cares about the world, and therefore man should as well—forms the basis of Berkovits' approach to Judaism, and is a consistent thread running through his writings. We may discern three important ways in which he develops and applies this idea: In *theology*, where God's concern for the world translates into a distinct view of the meaning of righteousness, holiness, and truth (ideas that Berkovits treats principally in *Man and God: Studies in Biblical Theology*, 1969, and in *Faith After the Holocaust*, 1973); in *ethics*, where his theory of morality is founded on the principle of human responsibility for what happens in the world, rather than on abstract rules of behavior (*Not in Heaven: The Nature and Function of Halacha*, 1983);* and in the Jewish conception of *politics*, in which the concern for human history requires the creation of an exemplary political collective, a nation constituted in order to set an example of righteousness (*Towards Historic Judaism*, 1943).

All three of these spheres—theological, ethical, and political—find their philosophical foundation, and their place as part of a coherent whole, in *God, Man and History*. The theological aspect is treated principally in the first half of this work. Berkovits begins by exploring the experience of God's concern for history, and treats it as the epistemological starting point for all discussion of Jewish philosophy, and as the basis for a Jewish critique of other systems of thought. He then shows how the content of the encounter between man and God, as depicted in the Hebrew Bible, establishes a relationship founded on mutual

---

* For a wider elaboration of Berkovits' approach to morality and Jewish law, see my introduction to Berkovits' *Essential Essays on Judaism* (Shalem, 2002), pp. ix-xxxvi.

regard and a shared concern for history. Finally, he addresses the
implications of his thesis for many of the classical problems of
theology, including the question of divine attributes, the meaning of creation, and the problem of evil. In Berkovits' view, the
central justification for the imperfection of the universe is not
to allow the possibility of freedom of the will per se, so much
as of human *responsibility*: The idea that man, as the pinnacle of
God's creation, may himself imitate the Creator by assuming
the burden of responsibility—by becoming, in essence, a creator himself.

This argument, in turn, sets the stage for his discussion of
morality and law. In the second half of *God, Man and History*,
Berkovits lays the foundations for a Jewish moral philosophy
grounded in divine concern and human responsibility. In his
view, the main streams of Western moral thought—from ancient Greece through Christian theology and continuing in
secularized form in modern ethics—suffered because they viewed
morality first and foremost as a matter of perfecting the individual's understanding and faith, out of a belief that if one's
intentions could be perfected, one's actions would readily follow suit. This approach, he argues, necessarily failed to produce
effective moral behavior, because it ignored the basic facts of
man's material nature. "Judaism," Berkovits writes, "does not
accept the facile optimism of the Socratic-humanistic tradition
that all man needs for the good life is the intellectual study of
the essence of goodness. According to Judaism, man judged by
his own nature is not as hopeless a creature as Christian theology would have it; neither is he as easily led to goodness as
humanism imagines." (p. 110) Man's actions, in other words,
frequently do not follow from his own reasoned understanding;
behavior is the product not only of reasonable or faith-based
decision, but also of blind habit. If goodness is to become a
central feature of human society, morality must be constituted
so as to have an impact not only on man's mind, but on his

entire way of life. In Judaism this is achieved through *law*, which trains man's material nature to seek and follow a higher order of things.

It is important to note, however, that law in Berkovits' view is not only the facilitator of a moral orientation. It also stands as testimony to the high position man is understood to hold in the overall scheme of creation. "The essence of the law is the same as that of the encounter itself," he writes. "It is an expression of God's continued concern with man... The law represents the highest affirmation of man, as well as his crowning dignity. By giving man the law, his Maker declares: I do care how he lives and what he does with his life." (p. 89) Having grounded Jewish morality in God's concern for humanity, and in the response of the individual to this concern, Berkovits advances this same argument in the sphere of the human collective, in the process creating the basis for a Jewish politics. If history is the central concern of religion, he writes, then one must recognize that history is made not only, or even principally, by individuals. Rather, history is the province of communities, and especially of peoples and nations. "For the deed to be effective," he writes, "it must not remain the act of an individual, but must become that of a community. The deed makes history if it is the materialization of the desire and will of a community of people joined together in a common cause... One cannot be a Jew only 'at heart'; one must be a Jew together with other Jews in history-making action." (pp. 138-139)

But because morality is not simply a matter of teaching but also of affecting habits, humanity requires not only a call to universal morals, but also the creation of a moral exemplar on the level of the human collective. Judaism requires the establishment of a "holy nation," a unified people, dwelling in its land and enjoying the benefits of sovereign authority, which seeks to represent the moral vision of Judaism at the level of national expression.

This understanding underlies Berkovits' entire approach to the Jewish people and to Zionism. To his mind, the greatest threat to long-term Jewish survival is exile, which, by rendering the Jews dependent on others and depriving them of the preconditions needed to fulfill Judaism's own ideal, distorts the meaning of their religion. "A people in control of its own life, capable of implementing Judaism by applying it to the whole of life, is a people in its own land. Judaism, as the religion of the deed, requires a people in its land," he writes. "The people alone can realize Judaism; in the land of the people alone may it be fully realized." (pp. 139-140)

This must be regarded as a significant statement in the history of modern Jewish thought, for in it we find an argument for a Jewish state founded on Jewish moral thinking, rather than on a messianic reading of modern history. For Berkovits, the establishment and survival of this state was not a foregone conclusion, but rather a vital need without which the Jewish people could not fulfill its most important mission.

In writing *God, Man and History*, Berkovits thus embarked on an effort with few parallels in the modern history of Judaism. This is not merely a meditation on, or an exploration of, a specific facet of the Jewish religion. Rather, it is a comprehensive construction of Judaism. This construction begins with first principles and proceeds, on the basis of arguments grounded in the classical sources, to examine the foundations of Judaism, while at the same time placing itself in contradistinction to the central premises of modern thought. This is an ambitious project, conducted by a thinker possessing a thorough command of both the rabbinic and philosophical traditions. For this reason alone it is worthy of being placed among the most important works of Jewish philosophy in the twentieth century.

★   ★   ★

This edition of *God, Man and History* represents the first in a series of reissued works by Eliezer Berkovits, published by Shalem Press in conjunction with the Eliezer Berkovits Institute of Jewish Thought at the Shalem Center. Established in 2002, the Institute seeks to encourage scholarship in Berkovits' thought through the publication and translation of his writings, the establishment of an archive, and the initiation and support of research on Berkovits' life, works, and philosophy. The current edition has been corrected and typeset anew; and the notes have been expanded to include full bibliographical information for the benefit of readers interested in following his scholarly leads. The index from the 1979 edition has been edited and updated.

It has been a great honor to participate in the project of bringing Berkovits' writings to a new generation of readers. My appreciation is owed to a large number of people who have given support and constructive criticism, including Zachary Braiterman, who coordinated the first panel discussion on Berkovits' thought at the conference of the Association of Jewish Studies in 2002; as well as David Ellenson, Emil Fackenheim, Howard Gilbert, David Hartman, Norman Lamm, Daniel Landes, Stephen Landes, Yosef Yitzhak Lifshitz, John Moscowitz, David Novak, Jay Ozerowski, Roy Pinchot, Aviezer Ravitzky, Marc Shapiro, Joseph Shier, and Tzvi Hersh Weinreb.

This book would not have been possible without the able efforts of the team at Shalem Press, most notably Yael Hazony and Marina Pilipodi. Marla Braverman and Yasmine Garval offered crucial assistance in bringing the project to fruition.

Finally, a special debt of gratitude is owed to the family of Eliezer Berkovits, and especially his sons, Avraham, Dov, and

Shimshon; as well as his granddaughter, Rahel Berkovits. The family has been generous in offering its time, support, advice, and materials, and has been an invaluable partner in this venture.

David Hazony
Jerusalem
Passover 5764/April 2004

I

THE ENCOUNTER
WITH GOD

CHAPTER ONE

Introduction:
Philosophy and Religion

The idols of the nineteenth century have disintegrated, and man is once again without direction and without a convincing goal. The calamities that have befallen our generation have bred disillusionment and cynicism. Some people, however, have started looking for a new anchor for their lives; they are searching for a purpose on earth. In their misery and confusion, men have naturally turned to religion.

Does religion hold the promise? It depends on how religion is understood, and on how it is approached. What is certain, however, is that in order to understand religion from the perspective of our own specific bewilderment, in order to approach it anew in the midst of our own perplexity, we must return to the sources. Old formulas have gone stale and are of little use. Only by returning to the ancient sources are we to discover the meaning that may save us this day. In what follows, such an undertaking will be attempted from a Jewish point of view. But before setting out on this journey, it is only fair to give some indication of the course we hope to chart, together with our reasons for choosing it.

Saadia and Maimonides, each in his time, undertook to guide those of their generation who were perplexed by the conflict between traditional faith and beliefs, on the one hand, and philosophical ideas and metaphysical concepts, on the other.[1] The doubters were to be offered certainty, and the hearts of the confused were to be enlightened and reassured. Both these giants of medieval Jewry accomplished their task by subordinating religion to the supreme authority of the intellect.[2]

On the foundations of Arabic Aristotelianism, Maimonides constructs a view according to which metaphysics and Judaism are ultimately identical. In this system, religion becomes the highest rung of the ladder of metaphysical knowledge. Human perfection, therefore, consists in "the attainment of rational virtues... the conception of ideas which lead to correct opinions on metaphysical matters."[3] The most important among such opinions is the knowledge of God, which therefore has to be based on metaphysics. But metaphysics in turn may be reached only by the study of logic, mathematics, and natural science.[4] The result of this philosophy of religion is that only a person who has mastered all the disciplines of human knowledge may then attain the knowledge of God. And thus we are somewhat surprised to discover that Maimonides, the preeminent codifier of Jewish law, maintains that the concentration of the intellect on God "is the form of service to God which is reserved for those who have apprehended Truth. The more they think about God and let their minds dwell upon him, the more intensive their service to him."[5] It follows inevitably from such a position that living according to the law is secondary to the intellectual service of God through contemplation. As Maimonides explains, the metaphysical apprehension of God generates love for God, whereas the observance of religious practices induces only fear.[6]

The conflict between religion and reason is in this way resolved—but so thoroughly that, as the result of the identification of the two, religion becomes absorbed by metaphysics. This raises a new and unexpected problem: If religion is so eminently reasonable, what need is there for revelation? Could not human reason have discovered the truths of revelation by its own efforts? The question puts all rationalist religious philosophy on the spot, for the answer can only be affirmative. Medieval philosophers expended a great deal of creative effort to explain the specific needs of man which require revelation, but all their efforts do little more than reduce revelation to an ancillary of reason. In essence, these thinkers adhere to the dictum of Augustine that while revelational knowledge is first in history, rational insight into the divine will is first in dignity.[7] Revelation is a kind of crutch for reason, which God in his mercy gave the human race in its intellectual infancy. It takes time for mankind to reach that height of enlightenment which makes the intellectual service of God possible. And moreover, what of "women and children" and the broad masses, who have no hope of ever mastering logic, natural science, and metaphysics, all of which are prerequisites for the knowledge of God? It was mainly for the sake of the unenlightened, we learn, that revelation was granted.[8]

This idea, having established itself, persisted in the history of philosophical thought practically up to our own day. According to Lessing, for instance, revelation offers nothing to the human race that reason, left to its own devices, could not discover; revelation just grants it to us earlier.[9] Immanuel Kant differentiated between natural religion, which is objective, and revealed religion, which is subjective. The two coincide when revealed religion is so constituted that man could arrive at it through the use of his reason, in which case revelation at a certain time in history and in a specific place could be most beneficial.[10] The

views of these two German thinkers, however, were only variations on an old theme: That of Augustine, who taught that
revelation was needed only during the early phase of man's
relative intellectual immaturity. The same theme was also taken
up more recently by Hegel, within the context of his own
system, when he said that "Philosophy was absolute knowledge
in the form of the idea, the intellectual concept; religion, on the
other hand, was absolute knowledge in the form of imagination."[11] The philosopher's tools are ideas; the populace's instrument of thought is its imagination.

These interpretations of the relationship between religion
and philosophy are reflected in the history of modern Jewish
philosophy as well. Nachman Krochmal, the Hegelian among
Jewish savants, affirms the identity of religious and philosophical
truths in the terms of his master: Philosophy and religion are
the same in essence; they differ only in form. Philosophy is
conceptual; religion is imaginative and emotional.[12]

In modern times, the unification of religion and philosophy
under the supremacy of reason found its greatest triumph in
Hermann Cohen's classic work, *The Religion of Reason Out of the
Sources of Judaism*.[13] The title is self-explanatory. For Cohen,
revelation is that which is eternally valid as the basis of reason
and its contents. Therefore, reason itself becomes the root of
the contents of revelation. The relationship between God, who
reveals, and man, who receives revelation, is thus an intellectual
one.[14] Man, as a rational being, is the "correlate" to the God of
revelation. On the other hand, the fact of the revelation at Sinai
is explained away as a mere political act, serving, as it were, the
practical purpose of committing the national consciousness of
the Jews to the cause of monotheism in history.[15]

It has rightly been said that this persistent tendency toward
a rationalistic interpretation of religion means that metaphysics
becomes the religion of the thinkers and religion the metaphysics of the masses.[16] It would seem, therefore, that those who

may be most in need of God—the philosophically untrained and, consequently, the more easily perplexed—have the poorest chance of ever knowing him and sharing in his salvation.

There may still be some comfort for "the masses," who, being unable to grasp the metaphysician's concept of God, miss nothing that might have been of much help to them anyway. But those who do follow the argument must ask: What can really be known about the God of the metaphysicians and the philosophers? He is the Infinite, the Absolute, the First Cause, the One. But how may the Infinite and Absolute be described? Theistic metaphysicians will answer that God cannot be described by any attributes of his essence. This is partly due to the nature of man. The Absolute, or the One, can have no attributes; and man, being finite, cannot grasp the essence of the Infinite. The divine essence is simply inaccessible to our understanding. Therefore, as Maimonides put it, "We can apprehend that he is, not what he is."[17]

Such a conclusion must have caused a great deal of embarrassment to theistic philosophers. They were able to purge religion of anthropomorphic descriptions of the deity; but what of other descriptions, such as God's omnipotence and omniscience, his love and mercy? Since obviously religion cannot give them up, how are they to be reconciled with the concept of the undefinable and unknowable nature of the Absolute? The theory of the negative attributes was supposed to have offered a solution to this problem. But this theory, as has been variously observed, contains a logical fallacy: It is a poor compromise indeed if, being unable to form an idea of God's essence, man must assign to him such attributes as omnipotence and omniscience so as to negate the possibility that God could be lacking in power or knowledge. As was already pointed out by Hasdai Crescas, the negation of an imperfection in God is in itself an affirmation.[18] All negative attributes are in reality positive ones. Or, perhaps more radically, one may say that all negation takes place on the basis of some affirmation. For example, only if I am familiar with the positive principles of arithmetic am I able to deny that five plus seven equals fourteen. What is more, such a denial must also imply the possibility of a further statement concerning the proposition five plus seven, one which is certainly positive.[19]

It may be well worth our while to try and understand the true significance of the negative attributes. The positive assumption of the *via negativa* is the all-embracing perfection of God. Now, such an assumption may be justified for a thinker like Philo, who was the first to conceive of the doctrine of the negative attributes. According to Philo, man apprehends God not by intellectual reasoning but by some "clear intuition."[20] He knows of the ecstasy in the presence of God. This is an actual and positive experience. It is true that Philo teaches, in conformity with the Bible, that no man can "set his gaze upon the Supreme Essence";[21] at the same time, he is cognizant of the mystical path that leads man toward God. It is as man actually approaches God that he comes up against the barrier beyond which he cannot proceed and still live. The barrier, however, is erected not by the finitude of the human mind, but by the blinding and consuming rays of the divine essence. The inapproachability is the direct result of the overflowing riches of the essence of the Supreme Being, and not just the logical necessity of a metaphysical concept. It is not that man cannot grasp, but that he dare not draw near. With Philo, the inapproachability of God is itself a positive experience of the Presence. It is the "affirmation" without which the negative attributes would be meaningless.

The theory of the negative attributes is without foundation, however, if one maintains that religious truth is essentially rational, and that God's existence is to be "demonstrated by arguments carried on in words."[22] Within the framework of such a philosophy all negation must be made on the basis of some affirmation. If only the existence of the Absolute is demonstrable, and not its essence, then there is nothing at all that may be predicated about it. Without positive attributes, there cannot be negative attributes.[23] How, then, was it possible for the negative attributes to play such a conspicuous role in the history of religious philosophy?

The attributes that alone could render the existence of God meaningful for man—his wisdom, justice, love, and mercy— were known to religion proper, but had no status in the realm of metaphysics. None of the arguments for the existence of God could prove them. Yet religious philosophy could not forgo them, for without them the purely metaphysical concept of God remained cold and empty. And so, believing metaphysicians proceeded to incorporate these exclusively religious attributes of God into their philosophical systems, insisting on giving them rational dignity in the form of negative attributes. As we have seen, however, they do not enjoy such dignity. They were borrowed from religion, together with their implied positive assumptions that alone make the negation meaningful. But they have no metaphysical status as such.

The truth of the matter is that the God of religion, who had been replaced by the God of reason, was thus reintroduced in the disguise of the negative attributes. The logical fallacy was overlooked under the pressure of practical necessity. The negative attributes are the stranger within the gates of metaphysics, giving notice that the essence of religion is in truth independent of metaphysics. The inconsistencies between them prove that, notwithstanding a proud and glorious history, the interpretation of religion which identifies it with metaphysics has failed. Indeed, the metaphysical Absolute leads to either Neo-Platonic or Spinozistic pantheism, or else, as Kant rightly maintains,[24] it is a mere Something about which nothing may be predicated.

"The Lord our God, the Lord is One" makes religious sense; "the One, the Absolute Being, the One is in us and we are in It" is a metaphysician's faith. The religious metaphysician's credo, based on the identification of the two, might well be expressed, "The One our chief metaphysical concept, the One is our God." Unfortunately, this is neither religion nor metaphysics.

However, we must not be misled into attempting to establish the independence of religion on the basis of a sense of disappointment with reason. Indeed, in the history of philosophy there seems to exist a natural alliance between skepticism and religious orthodoxy. As long ago as the second century of the Christian era, men of Tertullian's type adopted a thoroughly materialistic theory of knowledge in order to make room for revelation. As Wilhelm Windelband, one of the distinguished historians of philosophy, put it, the idea is that "the lower the natural knowing faculty of man, and the more it is limited to the senses, the more necessary does revelation appear."[25] Materialistic skepticism and a revelational religious doctrine are indeed strange bedfellows. Yet at all times there have been defenders of religion who felt that the less one depended on the power of the intellect and of the spirit within man, the better the chances for the affirmation of faith.

Nor is it only epistemological or metaphysical skepticism that "leads" to religion. More often, perhaps, the doubts have ethical relevance. Is man capable of the ethical deed, of the moral life? Can he do what is right beyond the self-centered drives of his senses? At all times there were those who enjoyed indulging in an ethical skepticism in order that they might more safely embrace a redeeming religious faith.

It is not our intention to explore further the efforts to justify the independence of religion by means of an epistemological, metaphysical, or ethical pessimism. For the trend has left no significant record in the history of Jewish thought. Pessimism and disillusionment might have been the psychological reasons Jews returned to God; Jewish religious thought, however, could never be based on despair with man and the world. Religion, according to Judaism, is no escape from the misery of this life. Neither the failure of reason nor the spiritual inadequacy of human nature is the justification of revelation. God is no *deus ex machina*.

In the present study, we will continue on a path that was pioneered by that "most Jewish of Jewish philosophers,"[26] Judah Halevi. To this day, he has remained the solitary figure among Jewish philosophers of religion who succeeded in recognizing the independence of the religious realm, while nevertheless maintaining a healthy respect for the faculty of reason in its own domain. He saw clearly the difference between philosophical thought concerning God and the reality of religion as manifest in attachment to God. Revelation and reason do not conflict in Halevi's philosophy; but neither has reason a chance to absorb revelation, nor need revelation defame the intellectual faculty of man—or denigrate human nature—in order to establish its own validity.[27]

In the discussion that follows, we hope to follow this example. To understand the true nature of religion, we shall look to religion itself. We shall ask Judaism to teach us Judaism.

CHAPTER TWO

Where Religion Begins

The entire structure that was built around the identification of religion and reason must now be seen as lying in ruins. It was originally erected on the foundations of the classical proofs for the existence of God; it is doubtful whether these proofs ever convinced anyone apart from those who, for reasons independent of the proofs themselves, were already convinced. Since Kant, moreover, the whole issue of proofs for God's existence should really have been regarded as closed for good, for Kant showed conclusively that the existence of God cannot be proved by speculative reasoning.[1] In keeping with the gist of Kant's discussion of the subject, we may say that from the perspective of man's finite condition, no logical deductions may be made concerning the existence of a Supreme Being which, in its infinitude, transcends all boundaries of human experience. If a First Cause or Intellect is required as the original "ground" of the world, it is the world of man's finite experience that requires it. But the requirements of logical deduction do not demand that the ground of the limited universe of man's awareness be an Infinite Being. One might well imagine that logical necessity would be more effectively appeased by the Platonic demiurge.

No doubt, the familiar proofs for God's existence may suggest a Supreme Being as a likely metaphysical hypothesis. But can a man pray to a hypothesis, let alone trust and have faith in it? The God of religion is clearly not a hypothesis.

Our purpose here, however, is not to discuss the limits of man's rational faculty. Indeed, nothing could be further from our point than to suggest that religion begins beyond the frontiers of the intellect. Strictly speaking, the limitations of reason are the concern of reason, not of religion. Whether speculation is justified in reaching beyond the realm of possible experience is a purely epistemological problem. In this sense, the proofs for the existence of God have done more harm to religion than is usually realized: The treatment of a problem of epistemology as if it were a question of religion has for many centuries diverted attention from the genuine foundations of religion.

It is a commonplace to say that biblical religion knows of no speculative proofs for God's existence. It is indeed one of the surprising features of the Bible that nowhere does it attempt to prove rationally that there is a God. This remarkable fact should be ascribed not to any naive piety on the part of the biblical narrative—the Bible is anything but naive—but to the very essence of religion. Whether God's existence may be proved is of little interest to religion.[2] Even if such a proof were irrefutable, it still could not provide a basis for religion. Some of the predicaments of metaphysical religion, discussed earlier, offer amusing illustrations of this point.

Medieval philosophy in particular labored heavily under the burden of the problem of divine providence. The cause of the trouble was the omnipresent Aristotle, who had taught that God, the pure and supreme intellect, knew only the purest of objects—that is, his own self. The divine thought thinks only itself.[3] This, of course, meant that the deity had no knowledge of the particular. Logically speaking, the idea implied the negation of providence, and its acceptance would have spelled the end of all religion. But Aristotle was *the* philosopher in the eyes of medieval thought; he could not be wrong. Therefore, an inordinate amount of intellectual acrobatics were performed in order to make Aristotle toe the line for Islam, Judaism, and Christianity, respectively. Medieval philosophy did not understand that the Stagirite's metaphysical First Cause was not the God of revelation. For while Aristotle's Unmoved Mover is the *cause*, it is not the creator. It may "move" matter, but matter is nonetheless coeval with it. It is unchangeable, and it "originates motion by being the primary object of desire."[4] It is apart from all sensible things; and with respect to intelligibles, being one in essence, it can think only itself. By its very nature, the Aristotelian First Cause is all by itself and for itself; it cannot, therefore, have any relationship at all to anything outside itself. But a god that cannot enter into some form of contact with that which is not itself need not concern man. Such a god is of no religious significance.

What has been said of the Unmoved Mover also applies to the Neo-Platonic One, the Absolute. The One is all-comprising. It is incapable of relationship with anything outside itself. Indeed, there *is* nothing outside itself, because the One is the All. Notwithstanding all the differentiations that the One may undergo, it cannot be the God *of* anyone, for there is nothing besides itself. Far from being able to serve as the basis for religion, the Absolute One renders religion meaningless. The logical consequence of perceiving the One as the supreme metaphysical entity is, as I have already suggested, pantheism.[5]

Religion's indifference toward the rational or metaphysical proofs for God's existence is presented neatly in the opening pages of the *Kuzari*. There Judah Halevi, perhaps with tongue in cheek, lets the philosopher of the dialogue make the Khazar king "see reason." How could God care about the intentions or actions of man? the philosopher asks. God, being perfect, is incapable of desiring anything of man. Desire is a manifestation of want and establishes dependence, but God is complete and at rest within himself. He is not in need of anything and is above knowing individuals. Halevi's philosopher has such an elevated concept of the Godhead that he renders his God useless for the life of the religious. Judah Halevi shows us convincingly that it is possible for man to entertain extremely exalted philosophical opinions concerning God, and yet—precisely because of such opinions—reject religion proper.

The foundation of religion is not the affirmation that God *is*, but that God is concerned with man and the world; that, having created this world, he has not abandoned it, leaving it to its own devices; that he cares about his creation.[6] It is of the essence of biblical religion that God is sufficiently concerned about man to address him; and that God values man enough to render himself approachable by him. In the Bible, God and man face each other, as it were. God wants something of man, and man may entreat God. We shall see further on how this is possible. It may, however, be stated at this point that, beyond any doubt, biblical religion bases itself on the possibility of a relationship between God and man.

How do we know of this relationship? How do we know that God is concerned, that he requires something of us, that he is approachable? Obviously not by metaphysical proofs that God exists, but by the appropriate proof that he is concerned and may be approached. We may discern what might be considered adequate proof in such a case by means of an analogy. How do I ever know that another person cares for me? Surely not by logical deduction, but by actually experiencing his care and concern. Care that is not expressed, that is not shown, that cannot at all be experienced by the person toward whom it is directed, does not exist. Care is a bond of actual fellowship between two people. How do I know that my neighbor is accessible to me other than by having been able to reach him in fact? A man knows of any relationship in which he may be involved only by the realness of his involvement.

Similarly, we can know of God's concern. A concern that is not experienced is a contradiction in terms. And thus we can know that God may be entreated by man by the actual experience of God's having allowed himself to be so entreated. We can be aware of the relationship between God and man only by having had a share in such a relationship. The foundation of biblical religion, therefore, is not an idea but an event—an event that may be called the encounter between God and man.

Bearing this in mind, we are now in a better position to understand the radical indifference of the Bible toward speculative proofs of God's existence. Whatever else may be proved by such a method, the event upon which religion is founded cannot. If the encounter is experienced in reality, what need for proofs? If, however, the encounter is not part of possible human experience, what use all proof?

Everything in the Bible is communication between God and man; everything is relationship. God spoke; God commanded; God called; God appeared—all reflect events that take place between God and man. In all these situations man experiences the presence of God, which seeks him out and addresses him.

Some of our religious metaphysicians are at times disturbed by the intensely sensualistic terms which Moses employs in recalling the events at Mount Sinai in the book of Deuteronomy. Again and again, the children of Israel are admonished, "Take care, lest you forget what you have *seen* and *heard*, and what has been *shown* to you." There is a continual reference to sense perception. And it is too simple to play down these "materialistic" descriptions of revelation by pointing to other passages in the same context, in which Moses warns the people against forming for themselves any visible image of God: "For you saw no manner of form on the day that the Eternal spoke to you in Horeb out of the midst of the fire."[7] This would be mere apologetics, and would miss the very meaning of the teaching. The text insists, of course, on the incorporeality of God; but it also stresses with equal fervor the importance of the sensory impressions at the revelation at Sinai. The full story is told by means of a paradox: That the invisible God revealed himself to the senses of man. This, indeed, is characteristic of biblical religion. The paradox is resolved in the great words: "It has been clearly demonstrated to you that the Eternal alone is God; there is none besides him."[8] It is not God who is shown, for he is not made visible; it is rather the knowledge "that the Eternal, he is God" that is shown. Now, "the Eternal, he is God" is not a metaphysical form of adoration; as such, it would be tautological. In the Bible, "the Eternal shall be my God" means that he cares for man and is concerned about his handiwork.[9] This knowledge that the Eternal is God cannot be gained by any intellectual insight. It must be shown to man. Moses was saying to Israel: At Sinai, you knew God—his presence, his word, and his command—by actual experience, in which all of your senses were involved. The knowledge that God was addressing himself to them was "shown" to them; it happened to them. The event itself brought the awareness of its own certitude.

That "the Eternal, he is God" is revealed in an event, that this knowledge was experienced—and that it remains capable of being experienced—is, of course, what is meant by the "living God," Judaism's incomparable discovery. The living God is God invisible and yet encountered; it is God, unlike the metaphysical deity, in active relationship with the world.

The reality of the encounter constitutes the independence of religion from any purely intellectual exercise. The encounter itself is revelation—in it God reveals his presence to man—but it is not teaching per se. Of course, it is hardly possible not to learn something of importance from the encounter. But its immediate significance lies not in what may be imparted to the mind, but in the event itself; namely, that it actually happens between God and this creature, man. The truly unexpected and overwhelming element in all of revelation is that God should address himself to man, that the two can "meet" at all. The fact that God speaks to man is the foundational religious concept, and is in itself of far greater significance than even the truth that God communicates. The most wonderful aspect of revelation, then, is not its content, but its possibility: Not the word of God, but the encounter itself.[10]

Once this is clearly understood, the age-old discussion of the relationship between rational insight and revelational truth becomes pointless. The encounter, being at the root of all revelation, is not a truth that is primarily communicated to man in the act of revelation, but a reality made manifest for him. Before anything else, it is not an idea conveyed, but a relationship formed. It is not a meditation on the Supreme Being that is taught, but a "fellowship" with God that is established.[11]

Nor is the need for revelation a result of the infirmities of human nature. For even if man could grasp the very essence of the deity, he would still be without God. The finest theories about friendship are no substitute for a friend. Intellectual understanding does not constitute fellowship with the Supreme Being. Thinking about God philosophically or metaphysically is not encountering him. But without the encounter there can be no Judaism. Without it, there is no religion.[12]

CHAPTER THREE

The Biblical Record

The Bible is not a textbook of philosophy or metaphysics, but rather the classic record of man's encounter with God. At this stage of the discussion, a crucial question is no longer to be avoided: How do we know that this record is credible? No doubt, everything hinges on the answer to this question. For if the biblical encounter did not take place, religion as we understand it becomes a worthless mirage, and it would be so much foolishness to pursue it any further. On the other hand, if the encounter did occur, it was undeniably the most important event in the history of man.

This question of the credibility of the biblical record really consists of two parts: First, whether the event of the encounter was possible; and second, what are the positive reasons for accepting the record as trustworthy.

It may be established that an event could possibly have taken place by showing that its occurrence implies neither a logical contradiction nor a practical impossibility. A logical contradiction is one that offends either of the two basic laws of logic, namely, the principles of identity and contradiction. In other words, a statement must first not be self-contradictory. Alternatively, a recorded event may be deemed a practical impossibility if belief in its occurrence would contradict some part of our knowledge which is safely derived from experience.

According to the former criteria, we can affirm that the biblical encounter does not represent a logical impossibility, for there is nothing in either the term God or the term man that would contradict the concept of the encounter. Indeed, there could not be, for, as we shall see, the encounter itself is a source of information about both God and man. We derive from the encounter the most relevant part of our knowledge and understanding of God; and the very fact of the encounter reveals to man one of the most significant aspects of his nature—that he is worthy of the encounter.[1]

Is the encounter, then, a practical impossibility? Is there anything in our experience that would exclude the encounter? In order to answer this question, we need not have a mastery of all knowledge derived from experience. It is sufficient for us to be able to grasp the nature of the knowledge that is gained from experience. It is a basic principle of all experimental science that there cannot be anything in our experience that may exclude *a priori* the possibility of the emergence of some utterly unexpected event. If such an event should happen, we would have to take notice of it and reinterpret the nature of experience in its light. It is true that with regard to future expectations, one may always take shelter under the leaky roof of probability and maintain that, judged by all past experience, the occurrence of a certain event is highly improbable. However, all predictions on the basis of probability theory must be founded on experiences identical—or similar—to the one in question.[2] How, then, can an estimate be made of the probability of the encounter between man and God? On the basis of our observations of the behavior of hydrogen and oxygen, it may be determined that the chances of their forming certain combinations are so negligible as to be practically impossible. But on the basis of what kind of experience could the probability of the encounter be determined? Could it be done on the strength of the fact that in one's own experience, one does not observe such a relation-ship? But the biblical record does not assert that these events happen to most people and at all times. What is recorded is that they did happen to some people at exceptional times. There is nothing in our experience to justify a statement that an event, never observed by us—especially when it purports to be differ-ent in kind from all other events in our experience—could never have taken place. Experience, by its very nature, may reveal only what is, but not what must or cannot be.[3]

At this point a few words are in order concerning atheism. An atheist, of course, cannot regard the encounter as being within the realm of possible experience. Where there is no God, there can be no encounter. The logical validity of atheis-tic reasoning, however, need not detain us for long. Kant has shown convincingly that the existence or nonexistence of God cannot be determined by speculative reasoning. If human rea-son is not allowed to deliver the proof for the existence of a Supreme Being—because such a proof would require reason's "transcendental" usage—neither can it provide, on the same grounds, the proof for God's nonexistence. The nonexistence of anything is not experiential and is not, therefore, provable without a "transcendental" use of reason.[4]

It might be useful to quote in this connection a modern logician's criticism of positivistic "metaphysics."[5] "Consider the proposition, 'There are no snakes in Ireland,'" he writes. "Surely, that is intelligible and presumably has meaning. But how can we verify it?"[6] Similarly we may say: The proposition that there is no God is intelligible, and atheists maintain that it has mean-ing. But surely it is no more easily verifiable than the opposite assertion that there is a God. Atheism is to be looked upon not as a reasoned philosophy, but rather as a purely subjective mood. Faith in God's nonexistence is as unproved as faith in his exist-ence, when the latter is held blindly. All that critical reasoning and experience may justify is agnosticism, which is the suspension of judgment. Atheism is a dogma, not a respectable philosophy.

If we consider the basic religious experience in light of the scientific attitude toward experience as such, we may recognize that the encounter may not be ruled out *a priori* as an empirical impossibility.

Science and religion are similar in their starting points: Both begin with an actual experience. "God spoke to Moses" is asserted as having been no less real an experience than, for instance, the law of gravity. There is, however, this difference: Whatever a scientist may hold to be true about acceleration can be tested experimentally, whereas "God spoke to Moses" cannot. The latter experience is not repeatable, and we are left with the biblical record alone. Now, this would indeed weaken considerably the credibility of the biblical report—if things could be otherwise. That is, if the encounter, as it may take place between one person and another, were repeatable at will, but its biblical variant were not, that would be a serious flaw in the reliability of the biblical record. However, what the biblical statement about the encounter seems to be lacking, as compared with a statement of scientific observation, is a result of what it has in common with all other human experience of what may be called an encounter.

Science deals with events as they occur in the external world of "objects";[7] the encounter, on the other hand, is an event that occurs on the most intimate level between one subject and another. Science, in order to succeed, must eliminate all personal and conscious elements from the field of observation, for the personal and the conscious are threats to the validity of the scientific method. Thus the scientist is an observer; he must never be a participant in the event he investigates. If he does not remove himself from his field of observation, he interferes with and upsets the data.[8] In the encounter, however, the opposite is true: The more intense the personal presence and the richer the conscious element, the more valid the experience. In scientific study, we deal with events in their objective relatedness to the outside world; in the encounter, however, we establish a relationship in the inner world of personal reality.

This difference may explain why the repetition at will of the religious experience is something that should not be expected. The experimental method of science requires a measure of control over the events to be observed and studied. Where such control is not easily established, the experiment is not readily duplicated. The important consideration for us is that the truthfulness of a scientific observation may be checked in exact proportion to the degree of control that the scientist is able to secure over the field involved. It is thus easier to experiment with inanimate objects, which do not require the involvement of a personal element, than with guinea pigs, which must first be caught, caged, and perhaps doped for the experiment. Likewise, experiments with free and conscious human beings are far less susceptible to repetition than those with guinea pigs, since with humans the personal element may not be eliminated by force, but must be freely surrendered.

Indeed, the event of a personal relationship, as exemplified by the encounter, may never be "controlled." Here, all control, whether exercised by one participant in the event over the other, or by an outsider over both, is itself destructive to the experience. Personal relationships may not be forced on anyone; they must be based on the continuous, voluntary consent of those involved. One may coerce human beings or bully them, but at that point all personal relationship ceases. We have already seen, however, that all scientific experience may be tested by the experimental method only in proportion to the control wielded by the scientist over his "material." This in itself explains why the religious experience of the encounter is hardly capable of repetition: Not only can man never possess such control over the divine Presence as to be able to make it available for experimentation; but if God, who does have such control over man, did wield it without consideration for the personal element in human nature, he would easily crush man. When man is not permitted to be himself, he cannot be encountered.[9]

Apart from the foregoing, experimentation is excluded from the realm of personal relationships for another reason. An experiment is never an original experience; it always contains an element of make-believe. It is not the actual event as it occurs in nature that we see in the laboratory, but a schematic replica, artificially created for the purposes of study. All experimentation begins with the premise, "Let us assume that..." Now, such a procedure is, as far as man is able to judge, advisable in the external world of things, but it is out of the question when dealing with personal relationships. If one wishes to know what friendship is, one cannot discover it by saying to someone else: Let us behave as if we were friends, and then let us observe our feelings for each other. One can know friendship only by the original experience. One must participate in friendship without reservation and without ulterior motive, or else one has to learn about it from others who were participants themselves and are able to tell about their experience. So it is with the encounter: It must be the original experience or it cannot exist. One may know of it either directly, by personal involvement, or indirectly, by the report of those to whom it happened. But there is no possibility of checking the truthfulness of the report by scientific experimentation. The encounter is not repeatable; one cannot experimentally discover the nature of God's relationship to man or vice versa. Where experiment begins, all personal relationship ends.

Thus far we have been discussing some of the differences between the categories of the personal and the objective. A continued consideration of these differences may demonstrate still further why the specific nature of the religious experience is inaccessible to control by the familiar scientific method. The scientist is an observer; as such, he looks in on his material from the outside. Whatever the events observed may be to themselves—that which may be called the "subject aspect" of reality—it is inaccessible to, and in fact not the concern of, science. On the other hand, whatever happens on the personal level of reality may be observed only from inside the event, that is, from the subjective aspect of those who are experiencing it. Here the scientist must be silent. Only the participant, the observer from within, may communicate his knowledge. Of necessity, his communication takes the form of a testimony.

The fundamental difference, however, between these two types of experience has yet to be addressed. The objective sphere of scientific interest is the realm of the general; the subjective sphere of personal experience is the realm of the particular. The general is the repetitious aspect of reality. Only on the basis of the repeated occurrence of identical events are scientific observation and prediction possible. Notwithstanding Heraclitus, science maintains that we constantly step into the same river of experience. It may assert this only by clinging to that which is common to all experience, to that which is general. This, in turn, can be accomplished only by the elimination of the particular from the purview of scientific interest. There can be no science of the particular or singular. But the personal is the most eminently singular; it is individual.

The personal is essentially unrepeatable. Coming around a corner, two human beings may collide. This may happen several times to the same two people. From the scientific point of view, if on each occasion the two move with the same speed and weigh the same, it is an identical event occurring again and again. However, the same collisions between these two people may also be considered from the subjective standpoint of each participant. We may ask: What has each of them experienced individually? It will then be discovered that these experiences are not a mere repetition. The first time the two collide, it is simply an accident; the second time, a strange coincidence. The third collision may lead to the striking up of a lifelong friendship (So sorry! We seem destined to meet), or to a fistfight (How can anyone be that clumsy?). It is only in the realm of the personal that we never step into the same river twice. For on the personal level, every experience affects the person and thus modifies for him, in some way, the significance of all preceding experiences. Two people never address the same word to each other twice, both times conveying the same message. The words "friend" and "beloved" do not carry the same meaning when spoken the first time as on succeeding occasions. Nor do two people ever embrace each other twice with the same significance. The first embrace, and the entire life experience of the two thereafter, color and modify the future of their relationship. And so it is with every experience in the category of the personal: Every instance or occasion of the personal is unique.

Just as there is no science of the particular, much less can there be a science of the personal. We may, therefore, conclude by saying that the encounter, being an event completely in the realm of the personal, is always original. No encounter is ever a mere repetition of a previous one; every encounter is unique. We may know of it when it happens to us, or through the testimony of those to whom it happened. Thus all knowledge about the encounter, unless it derives from direct personal experience, must necessarily be of the kind described in the biblical record. Furthermore, as we will see later on,[10] the very meaning of the encounter connotes an extremely rare experience;

the fact that it is not readily "observable" certainly provides no justification for its *a priori* rejection on the basis of a scientific theory of the nature of experience.

We may take it, then, that the biblical encounter contains no logical inconsistency, nor may it be ruled out *a priori* as an empirical impossibility. Let us now consider the reasons for its trustworthiness.

Biblical religion is history; and history is not taught by means of treatises on logic or mathematics, but through the records of eyewitnesses, or such as are based on them. Therefore, biblical religion, based as it is on man's encounter with God, could be established only by the testimony of the witness. The trustworthiness of the testimony depends, of course, on the nature of the witness. Who, then, are the witnesses?

First of all, there is what may be called the prophetic witness, the testimony of the unique personalities who are known as the prophets of Israel. In order to be able to form an opinion of their reliability as witnesses, we must recall the type of man they personified. The prophets of Israel were men without official position or authority, men without any vested interest in their activities among the people. They possessed great courage and were dedicated to their mission without reservation. Without consideration for their personal welfare and safety, they were at all times prepared to face, and if necessary to challenge, the established authorities for the sake of the word of God. Often they had to forsake their families and occupations in order to obey the irresistible call. They were men of sorrow who would not think of compromise; they were often a source of mockery to their own people, yet they would never yield.

These men, who risked everything without the thought of personal reward, brought a message to their people, a body of teaching whose validity and supreme ethical dignity remain unequaled to this day. Their linguistic vehicle was the prophetic style, whose majestic power and beauty have made the books of the prophets the unsurpassed literature of the ages. And since the style of a man is the surest reflection of the dimensions of his soul, we may say that the prophets expressed the highest ethical teachings of the human race in the noblest literary form, and exemplified the meaning of their teaching by their absolute commitment to the service of the message that they spelled out for man. Independent of all consideration of the source of the prophet's inspiration, the prophetic type is undoubtedly the highest among all known types in human history.

But the prophet speaks in the name of God. The encounter with God is the *conditio sine qua non* of all prophecy. Through the prophet, the word of God is communicated to the people. It is not necessary for us to assert that the prophetic message, as such, bears the marks of its divine origin. What we must consider is the nature of the prophetic claim itself: How the prophets themselves understood their message and function. Undoubtedly, they saw themselves as the messengers of God, as tools in his hands. "Thus says the Eternal" presupposes the encounter with him. Without the encounter, the prophetic claim is confounded and the prophet becomes a charlatan or a deluded dreamer. But to assume either of these possibilities of Isaiah or Jeremiah or Hosea or Micah, let alone of all of these men of unique greatness and spiritual authenticity, would be absurd. If these men were misleading their people knowingly, there is no honesty on earth. But if they were themselves deluded, then we have to conclude that the condition of man in general must be one of essential delusion, and one may not trust even one's own eyes.

Thus, even if we had to rule out the encounter with God because of its logical or empirical impossibility, we would still have quite a problem on our hands: Attempting to reconcile what then would have been the prophet's unjustifiable affirmation of such an encounter with his otherwise proven spiritual and ethical incorruptibility. But as we have seen, the possibility of the encounter may not be rejected *a priori*. What, then, prevents us from readily acknowledging the prophetic affirmation, except for a mere mood or a vague hesitancy of our reason? In the light of the powerful prophetic witness, such an attitude reflects a mere rationalistic prejudice.

Recalling the life of a Jeremiah, and conceding his genius of mind and spirit as revealed in his life and words, who may doubt that he was moved by an experience no less actual and real than any of our own, when he exclaimed:

O Eternal, you enticed me, and I was enticed,
You have overcome me, and have prevailed;
I have become a laughing-stock all the day,
Everyone mocks me...
Because the word of the Eternal has become
A reproach unto me, and a derision all the day.
And if I say: "I will not make mention of him,
Nor speak anymore in his name,"
Then there is in my heart as it were a burning fire
Shut up in my bones,
And I weary myself to hold it in,
But cannot.[11]

If words like these do not describe a true event and experience, all search for truth is futile; for then the very idea of truth is the product of a hallucination.

Nor does the witness of prophecy stand alone. Of far greater importance is the witness of Israel, the testimony of the Jewish people. Israel is not merely an ethnic group that also happens to hold certain religious views. Israel has been made a people by its religion.[12] We need not enter into a discussion with anthropologists on that account; their opinions on the tribal origins of the Jews are beside the point. Of course, there were origins; there always are. But whatever the origins, the Jews became the Israel of history because of what they held to be true about their biblical history with God. The story of the patriarchs, the Exodus, the revelation at Sinai, the journey through the wilderness, the prophets' struggle with the obstinacy of the people—for the Jews, these were not legends to which they gave some naive consent. They were events in their own history, which obligated the people for all generations. They lived either in conformity with these events or in rebellion against them, but at all times the events determined their national consciousness. All through their history, Jews were judged by their leaders and teachers, and often by themselves, in light of the biblical record of their encounter with God. Through the ages, they understood themselves in the light of that record; it set their standards of behavior, it formulated their goals, it expressed their historic purpose.

The Jewish encounter with God determined the entire course of Jewish history. Because of it, Israel never surrendered to other religions or civilizations. Acceptance of the meaning of their meeting with God shaped and preserved their identity. It was the source of the fortitude of their numberless martyrs. It has been their comfort, their hope, and their promise in all generations.

There was never a time in Jewish history when this was not the case. This is not to say that all Jews at all times adhered to the obligations that follow from Israel's encounter with God, but at all times there were those whose entire lives were determined by those obligations. And at all times, those who rebelled had to rebel against the meaning of that encounter in order to pass for Jewish rebels. But it was not through rebellion that this people was preserved: However far back we go in Jewish history, there never existed a generation in which some Jewish fathers did not teach their children how to live in loyalty to the meaning of the Jewish encounter with God. We are dealing here not with the dogmas of a church, but rather with events that for thousands of years have exercised the most powerful influence in the history of a living people. Jewish children were not taught: "These are the things we Jews believe in," but "These are the things that happened to us and made us what we are." Take away the encounter with God, and the existence of the Jewish people becomes inexplicable, its history inconceivable. "You are my witnesses, says the Eternal…"[13] Indeed, Israel itself is the witness. The existence, the history, and the survival of the Jewish people are themselves the most imposing witnesses to the Jewish encounter with God.

Nor is it of small significance that the witness of Israel bears a testimony that concerns not only the past. The encounter, as told in the biblical record, is unique in its nation-founding and nation-preserving significance. At the same time, Israel is the witness of the Eternal because there hardly ever lived a generation of Jews in which some outstanding individuals, and at times whole communities, did not have some immediate awareness of the Presence, and were not sustained by the direct knowledge of God's concern for them. The possibility of the encounter is never exhausted. Israel bears witness not only to the actual encounter in the past, but also to its ever-present possibility.

CHAPTER FOUR

The Paradox of the Encounter

We shall now attempt to analyze the nature of the encounter, as it emerges from the biblical record.

As we have already observed, the encounter is an actual experience in which all of man's senses are involved; yet it is certainly no material vision of the deity that is revealed.[1] There are signs, a voice, which convey with irresistible force the knowledge of the Presence, which itself is yet invisible. The knowledge is not derived, but immediate. The Presence is "felt"; it envelops the whole human being. It communicates itself with such overpowering certainty that no doubting is possible for those whom it confronts.

One may not always understand of what this sense of certainty consists, but often it is associated with an experience of danger. God's presence seems to be threatening; it imperils the life of the very person to whom it expresses itself. When Moses realized that it was God who spoke to him from the bush, the Bible reports that he hid his face, "for he was afraid to look upon God."[2] Standing at the mountain of Sinai, the children of Israel trembled with fear at the voice of God, which yet was conferring on them their greatest distinction. That their fear was justified, that they were in real danger from the very act of revelation, is confirmed by the words in Deuteronomy, addressed to them by their leader and teacher: "Did ever a people hear the voice of God speaking out of the midst of the fire, as you have heard, and live?"[3]

Numerous are the biblical passages that tell of the fear and trembling that seize the prophet at the moment when the divine Presence actualizes itself for him. This is not, however, because of the stern rigor that is supposed to be the hallmark of the "Jewish" deity. Such generalizations are proof that centuries of religious philosophy were not sufficient to help people understand the fundamental experience without which biblical religion is inconceivable. The peril resulting from "contact" with the divine Presence has nothing to do either with the sinfulness of man or with the judgment of the Almighty. It is something quite natural, almost "physical," if one may say so. A man wilts in the heat of the midday sun, or dies of exhaustion if exposed too long to the cold. Often mere lightning and thunder or the tempest of the elements frighten him. How, then, can he hope to stand in the presence of the source of all energy and power in the cosmos; how dare he approach it and survive? "Suppose a thousand suns should rise together into the sky,"[4] the Bhagavad-Gita asks, what would happen to our earth? Yet the "thousand suns" are a crude comparison, as all comparison must be, with God. By referring to him here as the ground of all power in the cosmos, I do not mean to suggest a material likeness of him. But whatever the unimaginable essence of the Almighty be, it does imply a concentration of power and energy (and who indeed would say these days what energy is?) that surpasses any imaginable such concentration.

The Almighty is indeed "a consuming fire";[5] not because he is angry with a sinful world, but because the potency of his being cannot be sustained by anything created. The Presence imperils men, not on account of God's will directed against man, but because divine nature is so charged with the vitality of being that its nearness naturally overwhelms all individual existence.

Thus, we are faced with a paradox. The God of religion, we have observed, must be a living one.[6] And a living God is one who stands in relationship to the world—that is, a God who not only *is*, but is also *for* man, as it were, who is concerned about man. We may know of the relationship only if it is real, if the divine concern is actually revealed to man. This is what we have called the encounter, which is the fundamental religious experience. Now we find that the encounter threatens the very existence of man. Without the encounter there can be no religion, but the encounter itself man cannot endure. There can be no religion without some active relationship between man and God; in the relationship, however, man cannot survive.

The paradox is resolved by God, when he "shows" himself to man. God, who reveals his "unbearable" Presence to the helpless creature, also sustains man in the act of revelation. The prophet Ezekiel, for instance, reports on one of his encounters: "And I fell on my face. Then the spirit entered into me, and set me upon my feet, and spoke with me…"[7] The key phrase is "and set me upon my feet." The prophet fell on his face because he was thrown to the ground by the force of the encounter. But in that condition of weakness, his ability as a messenger of God to Israel was taken from him. Only after the spirit had set him on his feet could God address him. The encounter crushed Ezekiel; but it was in the encounter that he was granted the strength to stand up and, notwithstanding the terror, face the Presence. God can meet man only by sustaining him against the impact of God's own Presence.

Obviously, not just any form of life sustained in the prophet will allow the encounter to take place. It is not enough to grant him a kind of life that may make of him some new creation, in the old external garb. The spirit has to set Ezekiel on his feet, so that he may again be himself. His own self must be returned to him; otherwise no encounter with Ezekiel per se is possible.

But Ezekiel may retain his personal identity in the encounter if God, in revealing his presence, protects the prophet against his "consuming" essence. All protection that shields the prophet, however, hides God from him. God can only reveal himself to man by hiding himself in the very act of revelation.[8] In the peril, which is implied (and yet restrained) in the encounter, God both reveals and hides himself. He reveals himself, that his concern for man may be known; he hides himself in the very act of revelation, so that the subject of his concern will not be consumed by the very knowledge shown to him. He reveals himself as a "hiding" God, so that man may live in his sight. As Isaiah said of him: "You are surely a God who hides himself; O God of Israel, the savior."[9]

We may now see more clearly what is implied in the encounter. It creates a relationship that is charged with ambivalence. In the encounter, man is threatened as well as sustained. The peril reflects the transcendence of God, which man cannot sustain. The danger is a reflection of the edge with which divine transcendence juts out into human experience. But man is also protected in the encounter. He is sustained by God, so that the encounter may be possible; that God may turn toward him, as it were. Notwithstanding the terror of divine transcendence, man is assured of God's nearness and accessibility.

Under the crushing burden of the Presence, man discovers his own nothingness before God, his complete dependence on him. But there can be no encounter with nothing. Man is therefore raised up again and granted strength to retain his individuality and to be himself. Unless there is man, there can be no revelation; unless man is permitted to be himself, there can be no religion. All relationship requires two participants; man as well as God must exist. In the encounter, the identity of

man must remain inviolate. Experiencing his complete dependence, man is at the same time granted a measure of independence. He is free to be himself because God cares for him.

Without that freedom, the relationship would be of no value,
for man would cease being a person. The encounter is significant because it happens between God and a person who is free
to be himself. The hiding God is, therefore, not only a "physical necessity," as it were, in order to protect the human being
against the "consuming fire"; it is a moral necessity too that he
should "hide," in order to preserve the personality of man,
without which no encounter is possible. Man may confront the
divine Presence only because God curbs, as it were, his transcendence. God "denies" himself in order to affirm man. By an
act of divine self-denial, man is made free to deny him. In order
to be encountered, man must possess his own self with a measure of freedom; and if so, he is also free to refuse the encounter.
But it is because of such freedom that the encounter becomes
a fellowship. The act of divine self-denial is the precondition of
the fundamental religious experience.

Thus, the encounter is significant also for what it implies
about the God of religion. In the terror, which is a hint of the
divine transcendence, God is revealed as the "Wholly Other";
yet man is able to gain a glimpse of the "Wholly Other" solely
because God, hiding his transcendence, makes himself accessible
to man. In the encounter, man does experience what has been
called the *mysterium tremendum*,[10] but he also hears the "still,
small voice" that reassures and affirms. The "Wholly Other"
reveals itself as the "friend," the sustainer and preserver. This is
of the essence of Judaism. God is far removed, and yet he is
near. "For though the Eternal be high, yet he regards the
lowly."[11] The combination of the idea of divine transcendence
with that of divine concern for man has found one of its noblest
formulations in the words of Isaiah, when the prophet declares:

Thus says the Eternal:
The heaven is my throne,
And the earth is my footstool,
Where is the house that you may build for me?
And where is the place that may be my resting place?
For all these things has my hand made.
And so all these things came to be,
Says the Eternal;
But on *this* one will I look,
Even on *him that is poor and of a contrite spirit*,
And trembles at my word.[12]

Bolder still than the prophets were the teachers of the Talmud, who possessed sufficient spiritual courage to make the daring statement: "Where you find the mightiness of the Holy One, there you also find his humility."[13] The humility of God is a frightening term; yet God's concern for lowly man cannot be explained in any other way. In the encounter, it is God's self-denial which "sets man upon his feet." One might say that only through divine humility is man granted strength of individuality to be able to endure, even briefly, the slightest measure of divine might. In the very terror of the encounter, man is affirmed.

Just as the divine self-revelation in the encounter is dual, so too is man's self-cognizance correspondingly dual. Man is threatened and affirmed at the same time. Through the peril that confronts him, he is bound to recognize his nothingness before God; yet in the divine affirmation, the highest dignity is bestowed on him: He is allowed into "fellowship" with God. A striking example of the dual significance of the encounter is found in the case of the patriarch Abraham pleading on behalf of the people of Sodom and Gomorrah. Abraham acknowledges his own position with the words: "Behold now, I have taken

upon me to speak unto the Lord, who am but dust and ashes."
Yet he does speak, and in the clearest terms: "Far be it from
you to act in this manner, to slay the righteous with the wicked...
shall not the judge of all the earth do justly?"[14] It is from God
that the patriarch derives the strength to face him; it is God
who granted this heap of "dust and ashes" the dignity of a
conscience, which must be asserted even when confronting
God. In the encounter, not only does God reveal himself to
man, but man is revealed to himself.

The dual nature of man, which emerges in the basic religious experience, found its classical formulation in the words of
the psalmist:

> What is man, that you are mindful of him?
> And the son of man, that you think of him?
> Yet you have made him but little lower than the angels,
> And have crowned him with glory and honor.[15]

Man, who is "dust and ashes" and yet "crowned with glory and
honor," is the corollary to God, whose throne is the heaven
and whose footstool is the earth and who yet looks on him who
is "poor and of a contrite spirit." It is the mightiness of God
that reduces man to nothing, and it is his "humility" that elevates man to a rank "but little lower" than that of the angels.

Through the encounter Judaism first learned of God, who is
Almighty and yet cares for man, Supreme Lord and yet a friend.
From his presence emanates assurance as well as terror. He is
King and Father. But since, as we saw, man's ability to survive
the terror of his presence is due only to the assurance of God,
it is through the Father that we know of the King. Therefore,
the Jew invokes God in the liturgical phrase "our Father, our
King."

And so is man, too, son as well as subject. The subject
cannot but tremble, for the sense of one's own nothingness

before the King may never depart; however, the son, the human personality redeemed from the state of dust and ashes and elevated in the presence of the Father, cannot but rejoice. The worship of the Jew is, therefore, one of fear and love.[16] Or as the psalmist puts it: "Serve the Eternal with fear, and rejoice with trembling."[17]

It is important, however, to distinguish between our interpretation of the prophetic encounter as the basic religious experience and the way of the mystic.

The encounter should not be confused with the mystical communion. The mystic's goal is the surrender of personal existence. His desire is to merge himself in the One, to pour himself into God, to be drawn into the All. The mystic finds his fulfillment in the extinction of his dignity through being consumed by the Absolute. For him individuality is a burden and a shame. Only the One or the All is real, and every form of separateness from it is an unworthy shadow existence. In the encounter, on the other hand, the original separateness is affirmed; in fact, it is granted its highest dignity by being sustained by God. The encounter may occur *because* the individual personality is safeguarded. Where there is encounter, there is fellowship; and fellowship is the very opposite of the mystical surrender of man's identity in an act of communion. Judaism is not a non-mystical religion; Judaism is essentially non-mystical because it is religion. The mystical communion is the end of all relationship and, therefore, also the end of all religion.

Judaism is essentially non-mystical because, according to it, God addresses himself to man, and he awaits man's response to the address. God speaks and man listens; God commands and man obeys. Man searches, and God allows himself to be found; man entreats, and God answers. In the mystical union, however, there are no words and no law, no search and no recognition, because there is no separateness.[18] Judaism does not admit the idea that man may rise "beyond good and evil," as it were, by drowning himself in the Godhead.

There is a natural affinity between mysticism and pantheism. All mysticism tends toward pantheism. Once the mystical union is completed, there is nothing left but the Absolute, in which all is contained. The appropriate worldview of the mystic is pantheism. It is his justification for devaluing individual existence, as well as for attempting to redeem it through return into the All. On the other hand, mysticism is the only available "religion" for the pantheist. His worship of the Absolute demands the denial of his own separateness from it. Thus, we are led to the Spinozistic *amor dei*; since nothing exists apart from the infinite, man's love for God "is the very love of God with which God loves himself."[19] One is inclined to agree with those who see in this the monstrous example of absolute self-love.[20] The truth, of course, is that where there is no separateness, there is no love either. Where there is no encounter, there can be no care or concern. The mystic endeavors to overcome all separateness; the pantheist denies it from the very beginning. Judaism, on the other hand, through its concept of the encounter, affirms the reality as well as the worth of individual existence. Judaism is not only non-mystical, it is also essentially anti-pantheistic.[21]

CHAPTER FIVE

Faith, Reason,
and the Encounter

The question may be asked: If the encounter is the fundamental religious experience, what does this imply about the nature of faith? What is its relationship to the encounter?

We have seen that the proposition that God exists, even if proved, need not lead to religion. Religion maintains not only that God exists, but that he is also concerned about man and the world.[1] Faith, therefore, requires belief not only in God's existence, but also in his concern. Originally, we know of the divine care for man only by actual experience. This thought gave us the concept of the encounter. While the encounter lasts, we know of God's concern beyond any doubt. But what of the time after the encounter? Does God withdraw himself from the world? Does he become the Absolute of metaphysics, for whom all involvement in life is inconceivable, until the next encounter? Such an idea would, of course, be absurd. It would destroy all meaningful religion. During the encounter man knows with immediate certainty of God's concern; afterwards, he knows about it by an act of faith.

In the encounter man is "shown" not that God happens to care at one particular moment, but that he is a caring God. Therefore, even after the actual experience of the relationship has passed, the knowledge remains with man that God does not withdraw, that he does not abandon man, that the relationship of concern is not severed even though it is no longer experienced. The knowledge follows logically from the encounter. But what is logic in the absence of the experience? Logically speaking, a caring God ought to care always. But we generally do not recognize his care and concern; most of the time God is silent, as if absent. Transcendental divine indifference seems to replace the short and extremely rare moments of the relationship in the encounter. It is here that faith has its place. Faith turns the theoretical consequences of the encounter into living reality. Through faith we know that even though God seems to be absent, he is present all the time; even though he is far, he is close at hand; even though he transcends all life, still we confront him every moment of our existence. Through the power of faith we know, as if by actual experience, that his gaze is always upon us, that no matter where we may turn, we are forever in his presence. The psalmist expressed this in the words:

> I have set the Eternal always before me;
> Surely he is at my right hand, I shall not be moved.[2]

The essence of faith is a sensitivity of the entire personality to the Presence, even when the realness of the Presence is not as directly evident as in the acute form of the encounter. The act of faith holds on to the encounter beyond its actualization. Thanks to faith, the encounter never passes; the Presence remains forever on the threshold of possible experience.

This function of faith is of vital significance for Judaism. We call Judaism a historic religion because it was constituted by a number of encounters between God and the patriarchs and prophets of Israel, encounters whose meaning has remained valid for all generations of Jews. Eliminate Abraham, Isaac, and

Jacob and their intercourse with God, deny the revelation at Sinai and the words of the prophets, and you have destroyed the foundations of Judaism. On the other hand, the encounter as the basic religious experience means that all religion must be personal. Unless God is accessible to me, unless I am able to confront him myself, unless he is concerned about the way I live and behave, however insignificant I may otherwise be, religion is not possible for me. But the confrontation between God and Israel, the Judaism-constituting encounters, occurred many centuries ago. How can they be personalized for me? It is true, these encounters are on record, and we have advanced reasons for the credibility of the biblical testimony.[3] However, to accept a recorded event as credible does not constitute religion, but belongs to the discipline of history. That God revealed himself to the children of Israel in the wilderness is history. As such, though a most unusual event, with far-reaching historic consequences, it would concern us only as a matter of information. Giving credence to the record becomes religion when the event is accepted as if what happened at Sinai had happened to oneself now. The problem of personalizing the public encounter in history is solved within Judaism by viewing God's revelation at Sinai as a continuing address to all the generations of Israel.

The solution is clearly expressed in the Bible in the well-known words of Deuteronomy: "Neither with you only do I make this covenant and this oath; but with him that stands here with us this day before the Eternal our God, and also with him that is not here with us this day."[4] It is noteworthy that the ancestors are not said to have concluded the covenant on behalf of their children. It is extremely doubtful that such a procedure could have been valid. The text insists that the oath and covenant were made with those too who were not yet born. The later generations did not inherit it; the covenant was originally made with them directly, as it was made with their forefathers. The need for so strange a concept derives from the very essence of religion. The covenant is the most intense form of the encounter. But the encounter must be real for me, or else it does not exist for me; and so it is with the covenant too. The covenant with my ancestors was concluded with them. As an event in history, it could not but affect the lives of their children as well; yet it could not be a covenant with the children. For me it is history, not encounter, that my forefathers encountered God. However, where there is no encounter, there may be philosophizing about religion, but there is no religion. For the revelation at Sinai to be revelation for me, it must be addressed to me. And so the covenant had to be concluded with all generations.

This could be done because, while the generations of the wilderness did pass away, God is timeless, and therefore the manifestation at Sinai is timelessly directed to Israel. The revelation at Sinai never belongs to the past; it never ceases to be. It is as if the divine Presence, never departing from the mountain, were waiting for each new generation to come to Sinai to encounter it and to receive the word. Judged from the aspect of God's relationship to Israel, as revealed at Sinai or in the exodus from Egypt, these encounters are ever-present events. The miracles and the signs, the thunder and the lightning are gone; but not God, or the message, or Israel. And so it is for the eye of faith to see what has been withdrawn from the senses, and for the ear of faith to hear, notwithstanding the silence.[5]

We may now say that while the encounter is the foundation of religion, faith is its edifice. Without the encounter, we could not know the God of religion, the God who is concerned about us and our world. With the encounter alone, we could not face the contradiction between what is conveyed in the encounter, which is God's concern, and what often follows after it, namely, his apparent indifference. Faith, in keeping the truth communicated in the encounter alive at all times, is the answer to the contradiction. Since the encounters are few and quickly passing, and since most of life is spent without their being granted to man, without faith the encounter itself would be like a tiny island of freakish fellowship with the Supreme Being in an ocean of loneliness.

It may now be advisable to take a closer look at the material, as it were, which goes into the making of faith. What is at hand to justify faith, according to our interpretation?

There are, of course, the memories of the experiences of the encounter. For those few people who themselves had the experience, the prophets and the saints, these are personal memories. The impression that the event itself made on them is indelible; it will easily change the entire course of a man's life. Yet even these chosen may doubt, not the existence of God, but whether the relationship has not been severed, whether God is still "mindful" of them. The quest of the pious for God is the quest for nearness to him, for fellowship with him. It originates in the anguish of the soul that feels the loss of "contact" as the result of personal unworthiness. Only one who has known such fellowship may call out, with the psalmist:

My God, my God, why have you forsaken me,
And are far from my help at the words of my cry?
O my God, I call by day, but you answer not...[6]

Only he who has learned of the nearness of God as a matter of immediate experience may exclaim:

Upon you I have been cast from my birth;
You are my God from my mother's womb.
Be not far from me; for trouble is near...[7]

The immediacy of contact can never be recovered outside the encounter. But the continuous recourse to the memory of it, as well as the quest of the soul for the renewal of the experience, causes one to develop an awareness of the Presence which, though withdrawn and silent, remains concerned.

This, however, is equally possible in the case of an entire people like Israel, whose memories of the encounter are mediated by its history. The memories of Israel are our own memories. The events to which they refer are our own history; they formed us and determined our destiny. And so we know of Israel's encounters with God as if they had been our own. As we delve into our memories, our hearts long for "the renewal of our days as of old" and for overcoming the estrangement. The longing is the beginning of the quest; it supplies the tension which sustains the soul in gaining awareness of the Presence through the act of faith, even when God is "hiding" from us.

The awareness of the divine Presence may not in itself be very conclusive; in itself such a sense may be completely subjective, a feeling to which nothing in reality corresponds. However, for him who starts out in his quest with the memory of the actual encounter, and the very real sense of estrangement from God which followed it, the awareness in faith of the Presence is like finding a lost treasure which is recognized by its familiar marks. In view of the original encounter, all faith is an act of re-cognition.

This idea may help us in discerning other sources from which faith may draw its strength. Any serious meditation on existence and the nature of being, any effort to attune the sensitive soul to the imponderable quality of reality, fills one with a sense of awe and mystery. Now, by itself, neither the awe nor the mystery is decipherable. On their own, they do not lead to God. Nature as such may justify both. Left to themselves, the experience of the mystery and the sense of awe are riddles without solution. But in the light of the encounter, we may occasionally recognize them as the traces of the Presence. The memories of the encounter are the key with which to unlock the secret of the mystery about us. They are guidance for the soul in quest of a lost fellowship. Only by the way of recognition may the mystery and the awe find their rightful place within the kingdom of faith.

The principle of re-cognition in the light of the encounter may also enable us to redefine the function of reason within the realm of religion. We have established the independence of religion from philosophy or metaphysics, but not for a moment did we mean to take recourse to any form of irrationalism as a source of religion.[8] The arguments demonstrating that reason by itself can never lead to the God of religion are themselves rational ones. This, we have shown, is not due to any skepticism concerning the value of the intellectual faculty, but to the nature of religion. Had God not actually revealed his concern for this world, it would be impossible for man to know about it. This revelation of the divine concern constitutes the independence of religion. That religion is based on an actual experience, and is not derived logically, does not make it irrational. For any non-dogmatic mind, once the credibility of the records of religious experience has been ascertained, the unexpected event of the encounter will expand the frontiers of the possible and modify accordingly the notion of rationality.

Once the encounter is made the starting point, we may understand the significance of a religious metaphysics and philosophy. All the known proofs for the existence of God yield no more than a "most likely hypothesis" that a First Cause, an Infinite Supreme Being, may well be assumed as existing.[9] This is about all that philosophy may accomplish for us, and it is not religion. But for the man for whom the encounter has laid the foundations of religion and who, possessed of its memories, is in search of the hiding Presence, the "most likely hypothesis" of a religious metaphysics becomes a source of continuous encouragement in the quest and a signpost for guiding him to the threshold of the Presence. The "most likely hypothesis" by itself has little convincing force, but if one comes upon it in one's search for the "lost" encounter, the hypothesis may be a potent factor in leading man to the form of re-cognition that he attains in an act of faith.[10]

We have discussed the intrinsic fallacy of the negative attributes of God.[11] But they do make sense for one who reaches the idea after the encounter. In the encounter, man is permitted a passing glance at the transcendence of God; it is that which fills man with insupportable terror.[12] As he then meditates on the essence of the Godhead, he may really acknowledge that it can be described in negative terms only. However, the negative attributes are revealed by the "terror," which itself is a positive mark of divine nature. The negative attributes, therefore, become an affirmation of the divine transcendence. In this way, against the background of the encounter, the negative attributes remain true to their logical implication, in that they do describe the divine essence and not nothing.[13] And we may again say that a soul steeped in the memories of the encounter may recognize in the negative attributes some positive features of divine transcendence at which man was permitted to glance in the terror of an actual experience.

In other words, in addition to the memory of the encounter and the longing of the soul for the renewal of "contact" with the divine Presence, the sense of mystery and awe as well as the philosophical quest for the ground of all being may serve as sources for the justification of faith. In themselves, as we have seen, neither the sense of awe nor the intellectual search will lead to the God of religion. But when re-evaluated in the post-encounter phase of man's experience, in the context of the effort of recognition, both may become significant forces in the constitution of religious faith.

At the same time, faith may never replace the certitude of the moment of the encounter itself. There is always an element of risk involved in faith. One may spend one's entire life believing, yet God may remain silent, and the loneliness of the soul may never be healed on this earth. To affirm, then, that God is "silent in his love"[14] is the highest creative commitment of which a man may be capable. The element of risk is the source of the tension that keeps the act of faith forever young. Because of the risk, one has to believe every day anew, one has to affirm again and again. Therein lies the essential significance of faith. Faith is commitment on behalf of God; it is a stand taken on the proposition that God is forever concerned about man and the world. It is a stand taken by man in freedom, in a situation in which the denial of God's existence need not be a logical impossibility. Only because faith is a commitment made in freedom is it a commitment at all; only because of this is it a continuation of the fellowship initiated by God in the encounter.

Commitment in freedom is the hallmark of fellowship. This may explain why the encounters themselves have to be rare and fleeting. We have maintained[15] that in the encounter itself, God may reveal his Presence only by hiding himself. The essential disparity between the transcendental "vitality" of the Almighty and the nature of man imperils man's existence. But even though in revealing himself God hid his power, the threat to the human personality would remain if the encounter occurred frequently. Frequent encounters need not cause the actual absorption of the individual in the Absolute, but they would certainly bring to naught his freedom of commitment. Two human beings meeting each other may or may not enter into fellowship; because of a general equality between them, they may accept or reject each other. With God, however, it is not so; one who encounters God cannot refuse him. Frequent encounters between God and mankind would give us certitude, but of such a compelling kind that it would crush our freedom to acknowledge him. In the interest of religion itself, the Almighty has to be a "hiding" God.

We may now, perhaps, even make peace with the idea that reason knows of no convincing way to God. In conformity with the requirements of religion, the intellect should be able to yield no more than a "most likely hypothesis" for the existence of God. All conclusive proof is a form of intellectual coercion. It is true, as we have argued, that philosophical proofs would still not give us the "caring" God of religion; nevertheless the logical necessity of valid proofs would considerably reduce the element of freedom and risk necessary for the act of faith. Because of the infinite inequality between the Absolute Being and man, the intellectual compulsion alone would undermine the value of man's commitment to God.

Religion does not reduce man to being a puppet of God; it elevates him to his highest dignity by enabling him to acknowledge God in free commitment. The "fellowship" is initiated by God in the encounter; it is sustained after the encounter in the ever-renewed act of faith by man. To make this possible, God must hide: During the encounter, to safeguard man's own survival; in history, to protect the spiritual independence of man in making his decision for God; and, finally, God must remain elusive to the conclusive grasp of reason so that man may retain his intellectual freedom. Where there is compulsion, there can be no fellowship.

CHAPTER SIX

God Encountered

One of the major problems of all philosophy of religion is that of the divine attributes. It is inconceivable that man's understanding should be able to penetrate to the essence of the Infinite. It is, therefore, unclear how the divine being may be described, except in a formula such as "the Eternal, he is God."[1] But what is really gained by this apparent tautology?

We shall here consider the "information" that is conveyed about God in the encounter, that which is revealed to man in the basic religious experience.

No doubt, the most significant thing that we learn from the experience is that God is present *for* man,[2] that he stands in relationship to this world. The relationship is fundamental to all religion; but it can only be known if it has been "shown" to man.

We are told in the Bible that God is One.[3] It is not the Neo-Platonic One that is thus revealed. We know nothing about the One of Neo-Platonism. In the Bible it is the Eternal our God, known from the encounter, the Eternal who led us out of the land of Egypt, who spoke to us at Sinai, who was with us in our wanderings through the wilderness, a "familiar" God, of whom it is affirmed that he is One.[4] But his oneness, too, has to be revealed, or else it could not be known. The philosophical reduction of Being to the One is not at all convincing. There is no end to the possibilities of explaining the ground of reality either by the principle of unity or by that of multiplicity. In metaphysics, the conflict between the one and the many remains forever unresolved. The intellect's aspiration to discover unity and order in the midst of multiplicity is an endless adventure. The achievements of this adventure are unceasingly challenged by the continually emerging elements of disunity. At all times, new waves of the primordial chaos seem to be welling up from the deep to mock man's neat discovery of order in the universe. Especially when judged from the angle of amoral purpose, Being seems to be much more readily explainable as the multiplicity of interests than as unity. Individual as well as historic experience appears to provide ample bias toward the Manichaean philosophy of a dualistic universe, in which two antithetical principles are locked in a perennial struggle for dominion. Furthermore, even if the principle of oneness could be conclusively established, we would know that the ground of reality was one only insofar as reality might be encompassed by our experience and our intellect. But "our" reality is of necessity limited, and, therefore, the One thus gained would be finite itself.[5] We would never know that "there is none else beside him."[6] The God of the Bible, however, is the only One.[7] We cannot know that he is alone in his oneness, except as it is "shown" to us by an act of revelation in an actual encounter.

As to the essence of God itself, the notion of its transcendence is undoubtedly communicated. However, transcendence is not conveyed as a concept or as a clearly definable metaphysical idea, but in an experience of its realness in which the entire human being participates. It is the experience of the divinity as "Wholly Other" which is the source of the *mysterium tremendum*.[8] The experience of divine transcendence is granted to man in the moment of terror, which is inseparable from the encounter.

The transcendence of the Supreme Being is thus touching man, as it were, in a moment of excruciating, overwhelming awe. Man receives no hint of the further reaches of divine transcendence. This, of course, could not be otherwise. Man could never survive the burden of an encounter with the realness of the Infinite, or even the mere vision of the full compass of the Absolute. Infinitude and Absoluteness are intellectual concepts; it is not possible to experience their corresponding reality. On the other hand, the fleeting breeze of transcendence, which shakes man in the encounter for a quickly passing and saving moment, is an experience. For this reason, all biblical descriptions of the transcendent nature of God are couched in terms of finite experience.

In order to illustrate the point, we quote one of the classical passages of prophetic elaboration of divine transcendence, in the book of Isaiah:

> Who has measured the waters in the hollow of his hand,
> And meted out heaven with the span,
> And comprehended the dust of the earth in a measure,
> And weighed the mountains in scales,
> And the hills in a balance?...
> Behold, the nations are as a drop in the bucket,
> And are counted as the small dust of the balance;
> Behold, the isles are as a mote in weight...
> All the nations are as nothing before him;
> They are accounted by him as things of naught
>   and vanity...
> Do you not know? Do you not hear?
> Has it not been told you from the beginning?
> Have you not understood the foundations of the earth?
> It is he that sits above the circle of the earth,
> And the inhabitants thereof are as grasshoppers;

That stretches out the heavens as a curtain,
And spreads them out as a tent to dwell in...
To whom then will you liken me, that I should be equal?
Says the Holy One.[9]

Now and then one comes across philosophical writers who
point to the naivete of passages such as this one. Metaphysically
speaking, the Absolute is in a category of its own. It is indeed
incomparable, but not because it is much bigger and much
more powerful than anything else, but because it is *essentially*
unlike anything else. Notwithstanding such criticism, the entire
passage is aglow with religious inspiration. It is not meant to be
read as a metaphysical dissertation on the subject of the Infinite,
but as an interpretation of the moment in which transcendence
touches man in the actual encounter. Since it is a positive
experience of God as Wholly Other, the incomparability of the
divine being is described in comparative terms, relative to experience. It is not an attempt to encompass the Absolute, but to
convey the vision of divine transcendence as it takes shape,
heavily veiled, at the transitory moment of its contact with the
finite realm. Strictly speaking, the Absolute per se is not a
subject of religion. The focus of all religion is the Absolute in
its relationship to man and the world. It is the moment of
transcendence in its relatedness to man which is described in the
biblical passage in terms of "comparative" incomparability.

If, however, the notion of the Absolute itself cannot be
conveyed in the encounter, how does religion acquire the idea?
In the answer to this question, we should recall what has been
said above regarding the function of reason in religion. In the
question of attributes we are presented with yet another example of that function. The religious thinker starts out with a
number of certitudes which are germane to religion. Religion
has shown him that God is One, and that "there is none else."
He also has definite cognizance of the "edge" of divine

transcendence jutting into the sphere of human experience. If he then, impelled by intellectual curiosity, inquires into the logical or metaphysical consequences of the fundamental religious experience, he may discover the entire discipline of a philosophy of religion. He will find that the One has to be thought of as incorporeal; that if "there is none else beside him," then God must be infinite. These insights may further lead the religious thinker logically to the idea that the transcendence of an incorporeal, infinite being has to be absolute. In this way, we may be able to readmit a great deal of the philosophy of religion, which we were at first compelled to reject.[10] There is no path from the metaphysical Absolute to the God of religion, but there is one from the revealed God of religion to the Absolute of metaphysics and its incorporation into the body of religious affirmations.[11]

The combination of the religious experience with philosophical reasoning will therefore yield the incorporeal, infinite, and absolute Godhead. But with it we seem to have slid back into the rut of the "negative attributes." The essence of the one God remains unexplored. What is being asserted is the denial of multiplicity, of corporeality, of finitude or dependence in the divine essence. We have seen that once we reach the negative attributes coming from the encounter, their metaphysical meaninglessness is redeemed by meaning and significance. In the post-encounter phase of human experience, they do describe quite "positively" the inconceivable essence of the Supreme Being, which is no longer an unknown "stranger" to man. The rut of all religious metaphysics is thus avoided; nevertheless, this solution to the problem still offers too meager a fare to justify the requirements of the logic of religion.

It was clearly appreciated in the history of religious philosophy that the negative attributes by themselves were unable to sustain a Godhead which would justify religion. In order to remedy the situation, the negative attributes of essence were supplemented by the positive attributes of divine action.[12] These attributes of action were usually seen formulated in the passage of Exodus where God is described as "merciful and gracious, long-suffering and abundant in goodness and truth; keeping mercy to the thousandth generation."[13] But the blight of the negative attributes is cast over even attributes of action. Can religion, for example, accept the interpretation of Maimonides when, explaining this passage, he says that "what is meant here is not that God possesses moral qualities, but that he produces actions similar to the ones emanating from ourselves by virtue of such moral qualities, or rather states of the soul"?[14]

Whatever might be said in favor of the negative attributes when discussing such metaphysical concepts as unity, omniscience, or omnipotence, the idea is untenable from the religious point of view when one deals with the moral attributes of the deity. According to Maimonides, the psalmist's claim that "as a father has compassion upon his children, so was the Eternal merciful to those who feared him"[15] is not to be taken literally. And when in the book of Malachi it is said: "And I shall be merciful to them as a man is merciful unto his son,"[16] the words have, according to the same school of thought, only some symbolical meaning. "Of course," says Maimonides, "God is not experiencing the feeling of affection or tenderness, but such actions as a father will do for his child through pure love, compassion, and affection do emanate from God with regard to his favorites, though they are not caused by affection..."[17] Now, this is an opinion that denies the most precious and intimate aspect of God's relationship to the world and to man. The negative attributes will never do. Religion cannot forgo the love and the mercy of God, or even his justice and anger. Such attributes have to be related to him in a positive sense, or else there is no basis for a living God of religious relevance.

What Maimonides denies God, namely affection and tenderness, are of the very essence of the encounter. As we have observed, the Supreme Being seeks out man in order to encounter him, as a manifestation of his care and concern for man; indeed, as a revelation of his affection. God upholds man in the encounter, hiding himself for man's sake, protecting man against the peril of divine transcendence so that man may endure him and, in this way, know him. This is an act of divine love. And so we maintain that the "thirteen dispositions" cited in Exodus do indeed describe God himself, expressing positive aspects of his being. God does not act *as if* he were "merciful and gracious, long-suffering and abundant in goodness"; God is as he is here proclaimed. He is a caring God.

It is, however, to be noted that in the "thirteen dispositions" no attempt is made to describe God in his absoluteness. All the "dispositions" are related to man. We have seen that the Absolute as such is no concern of religion, but only the Absolute in its relatedness to man. It was, therefore, natural that Moses' quest for knowledge of "the ways" of God should have been answered by the exposition of the nature of divine relatedness to man. The attributes of the God of religion are, of necessity, relational attributes.

CHAPTER SEVEN

The Absolute Versus God

Only relational attributes of God are the genuine concern of religion. However, we still must explain how such attributes are imaginable. Is the Supreme Being indeed subject to affections? Are not love and mercy and justice anthropomorphic impositions on the Absolute? If God is capable of affections, he must also surely be subject to change; but are not the Absolute and the Infinite unchangeable?

We need not enter into an elaboration of these questions, which have already been thoroughly explored in the history of religious philosophy. It seems, however, that the attempted solutions to the problem of the attributes were a waste of effort; most philosophers were treating the symptoms instead of addressing the malady itself. For the problem is not really whether God is capable of affections or whether his essence may be grasped by finite minds. The problem is that there exists a genuine contradiction between the concept of God and that of the Absolute. God is conceived in relationship to the world. In religion, he confronts man; he is a subject—and, at times, an object—*for* man. God is to be known in some way, or else the confrontation would be impossible. He must therefore have attributes. The Absolute, on the other hand, is the highest principle of unity; it is all-embracing and self-contained, and outside all possible relationship. The Absolute is Being in perfect Oneness, and therefore incapable of any distinctive attributes.[1]

It was seldom appreciated that the problem was not how God could be known by man, but—since God was identified with the Absolute—how he could be capable of relationship. If relationship were possible, attributes would follow as a matter of course. But if relationship were not conceivable, the question of attributes would lose all meaning. Without a God who relates to the world of man in some way, there is no religion, and one is free to follow the logic inherent in the concept of the Absolute and to reject all attributes. For the Infinite One, indeed, has no attributes.

If, therefore, the primary issue is not the problem of the attributes but that of relationship, we should focus our attention on the original point of contact between God and the finite world. This point of contact should be recognized in the act of creation. Creation is, after all, an act of relationship: As the Creator, God confronts his work. The term "creator" is thus the first and fundamental attribute. Creator and creation confronting each other is the first encounter in the universe. Very likely, if creation proves an acceptable notion, all other relational attributes will begin to seem plausible as well.

The conflict between the God of religion and the metaphysical Absolute is nowhere to be understood more clearly than in the examination of the question of creation. The Absolute, it is understood, is completely at rest within itself; it is incapable of creation. This insight has been responsible for some of the major trends in the development of metaphysical thought. It is, for instance, at the root of the emanation theory in Neo-Platonism, according to which the One, free of all want and desire, is incapable of volition and action. The world, therefore, could not have come into being because of creation, which requires an act of will, but is rather the result of the natural overflow of the infinite substance, an emanation of its limitless brilliance. In other words, the birth of the world occurs automatically, through the force of material causation. Thus, Neo-Platonism claims, in effect, that the universe has no identity of its own. Everything is emanation; everywhere there exists only divine substance, albeit in various forms of degradation.[2] Spinoza carried this idea to its logical conclusion: The Infinite, once admitted, is bound to claim all reality for itself and to squeeze everything else out of existence. There is thus no cosmos, only the infinite substance that is identified with God. In turn, the divine substance, because it is infinite, cannot be limited by anything else; therefore, nothing exists besides God. Spinoza's acosmic pantheism represents the Absolute in its fullest consistency. Logically speaking, then, there is no path from the Absolute to a world of separate, finite reality.[3]

A great deal of fruitless travail might have been avoided, particularly in medieval religious philosophy, had the full implication of the idea of the Absolute been understood. Lacking an appreciation of the conflict between the concept of the Absolute and that of God, religious philosophers maneuvered themselves into an intellectual cul-de-sac. On the one hand, they accepted from religion the dichotomy of God and world; on the other, they identified God with the Neo-Platonic or metaphysical Absolute, which permits no world besides it.[4] We may thus discern one of the most striking inconsistencies in the classical philosophy of religion: While religious thinkers balked at the thought of positive attributes, they readily embraced the idea of creation. In reality, however, both attributes and creation are essential for God, just as both must be equally excluded from the concept of the Absolute. Since the problem of the attributes was really the problem of the possibility of relationship in disguise, all attention should have been concentrated on the original act of relatedness, namely, creation. Unfortunately, philosophers of religion were too busy proving that the world was created to recognize that their concept of God as the Absolute was incapable of creation.[5] The prototype of all attributes is that of the creator. If God is the creator, he desires the world to be. But if he desires the world, why could he not be merciful to his creation "as a father has compassion upon his children"?

Needless to say, only the God of religion can be the creator of the cosmos. He did exactly what is inconceivable of the Absolute; without having done it, he could not be the God of man and the world. Without man and the world, it is true, he might still be the Absolute; but the Absolute is not God. From where, then, does religion derive its concept of creation?

Like the proofs for the existence of God, so, too, do the proofs for the creation of the world carry little conviction. We take it for granted that creation cannot be proved either by logical reasoning or from experience. As we said of the proofs for God's existence,[6] we may now say of creation: The question of whether it can be proved, philosophically or metaphysically, is in itself of small religious interest. In the history of the philosophy of religion, the idea of creation served mainly as an explanation for the existence of the world. Accordingly, creation is the cause of causes, a kind of a first cause that replaces the Unmoved Mover. As such, the idea explains how the world came into being. God did it. Very interesting, no doubt. But, so what? An explanation that provides nothing more than an interpretation of the original cause of the cosmos is not religion but cosmology. The religious idea of creation is not so much the answer to the question, "How did the world come to be?" as it is to the question, "What is the world?" Creation is not just a first action that generated the chain of events through which the world appeared, nor is it only the cause that initiated it all; it is the cause as well as the "ground," or, perhaps more accurately, the essence, of all being.

The world is God's creation—this is the most significant statement that may be made about the world. It not only explains how the universe came about, but also describes the fundamental quality upon which its continued existence depends.[7] We may therefore say that everything that exists belongs to God as his creation, and has God as its creator.[8] Not surprisingly, we once again find ourselves speaking in terms of relationship. For creation is in fact the unsevered bond between reality and its divine origin.

How do we know of this bond? All basic religious knowledge is derived from the encounter, and so it is with the idea of creation as well. The element of divine transcendence that is present in the encounter inspires in man a sense of utter dependence, which verges very nearly on the annihilation of individual identity. At the moment of the encounter, man knows himself to be helplessly delivered into the palm of the Almighty; he recognizes his nothingness. This experience reveals the "Wholly Other" as the master and lord, the source of existence, the cosmological cause, as it were, of the world. But in the final outcome, man is not nothing; he does not perish in the encounter. He survives, he comes to learn, through God; because God sustains and upholds him. The "Wholly Other" becomes the friend and companion; man, who is imperiled in the encounter, is also affirmed.[9] As a creature aware of his complete dependence on God to the limits of personal extinction, and yet confirmed in his personal identity by God's care, man comes to know himself in the encounter as belonging altogether to God. This is the full sense of the *kreaturgefuhl*; it conveys not only separation, but also belonging. To be means to be a mere creature, only "dust and ashes"; and yet, to be a creature still means to be oneself by the mercy of God, and to belong to him—to know that as my Creator, he is my God. Thus, understanding by means of the encounter that man and his world are God's own, man understands the religious idea of creation. Creation, as the unsevered bond between existence and its divine origin, is the prime manifestation of God's concern, which we found in the encounter.

We may now, perhaps, understand why the question that served as the starting point for the present discussion no longer poses as serious a problem as it appeared at first. The person who takes his stand on the ground of religion gains his most important knowledge of God through the experience of the encounter. In the encounter, he learns that the one God, besides whom "there is none else," relates with affection and care to the world that is God's. At the same time, if this person is interested in metaphysical inquiry, he may deduce logically from such knowledge that the One God should be thought of as infinite and absolute.[10] Then, when the question is asked, "How may divine absoluteness be reconciled with a caring Creator who maintains a form of relationship to his work?" the religious person may readily answer, "That, I do not know." His ignorance on this point will in no way affect the validity of his position. For him, God has become real in the encounter. What he is able to conclude from the encounter makes the identification of God with the Absolute not real and immediate, but a logical inference. The contradiction between the unrelated Absolute and the God of the relational attributes cannot undo either the fact of the encounter or the validity of the logical inference from it. Notwithstanding the contradiction, man *has* experienced God's care for man in a manner that causes him to reason that this same God is absolute and infinite. In spite of the conflict, then, neither the experience nor its logical implication may be denied.

If, then, there is a contradiction between the fact of the encounter and its logical consequences, this must be due to our own ignorance. Actually, we may almost put our finger on its source. The encounter with man can materialize only if God hides himself. This is the fundamental paradox that makes religion possible: In order to reveal himself, God must veil his presence.[11] The hidden God is not the unknown God; on the contrary, only the hidden God who reveals his concern for man may be known. Whatever is "shown" to man in the encounter may be so revealed to him only when he is guarded by a "protective wall of ignorance." Is it not reasonable, then, to conclude that the resolution of the conflict between the God of the encounter and the logic of some of its elements—which leads from God to the Absolute—is most likely to be found behind the wall of ignorance, beyond which we dare not advance? Since only the veiled Presence confronts us, should we not simply learn to expect difficulties of this nature when attempting to interpret the ultimate implications of the experience?

The position of the metaphysician, however, is different. He cannot start with the realness of God, for he has already accepted the idea of the Absolute. Once he has done that, his religion is doomed. He may not plead ignorance; with the Absolute as his starting point, he will never arrive at the world and the realness of individual identity. For the metaphysician of the Absolute, there is no actual confrontation between God and world, and as a result, the problem of relatedness is not even allowed to arise. Before pleading ignorance to the question of how the God of the world may be identical with the Absolute, which is incapable of any relationship, he would have to establish the separate identity and realness of the cosmos. With the concept of the metaphysical One, however, this can never be achieved. As we have seen, there is nothing outside of or apart from the Infinite One of metaphysics.

Notwithstanding the "protective wall of ignorance," we may push our quest to understand God's relationship to the world one step further.

Creation, as the bond between God and the world, necessarily involves God in the destiny of the world. This was already addressed earlier, when we noted that in the encounter, the Supreme Being is revealed as the caring God.[12] To care is to be involved. God's involvement in the world is the source of all anthropomorphisms: The God who cares loves; because he cares, he punishes and forgives as well. All this is no less understandable than the fact that he creates. Involvement, motivated by concern, is by its nature "anthropomorphic." And since God's involvement in the destiny of man is the precondition of religion, "anthropomorphism" is indeed inseparable from it. That God cares is no mere allegory, but a statement of fact, which one makes on the basis of the actual experience of the encounter. If so, we are here fully justified in putting the term anthropomorphism in quotation marks: The concept no longer indicates that man ascribes human characteristics to his idea of God, but rather that in his experience, divine intentions and actions whose likeness may also be found among men were revealed to him. That similar intentions and actions are also found among men does not make them less true of the nature of God's involvement with us; rather, they become all the more valuable and precious in us. True anthropomorphism is the making of God in man's image, and is certainly to be rejected as idolatry. But the discovery of the likeness in men of the "relational attributes" of God merely reflects the truth that man is formed in God's image.

We may take the discussion yet another step further. God's involvement with the realm of finite reality is imaginable only as an act of divine "self-limitation." God, despite his transcendence, bends down to the world of finitude. He "humbles" himself,[13] as it were, in order to relate himself to the world. He "reduces" himself so that he may enter into the narrow straits of a relationship with finite existence. But the fundamental act of divine involvement is creation itself. We will, therefore, have to view it as the basic deed of divine self-limitation: God creates the world of finite being by curbing the full manifestation of his essence and power. In order to create, he must restrain his infinite potency to such a degree that nothing may issue from the work of his hand that surpasses the boundaries of a finite universe. Creation is thus only conceivable as an act of divine self-abnegation. God is involved in the destiny of finite being as the result of an act of self-denial.[14]

This is, perhaps, the fuller meaning of the concept of the "hiding" God. God not only veils his presence so that it may be endured by man; he denies his essence so that the world of finitude may come to be, and he himself may remain involved in it. An act of self-limitation is thus the premise of creation, as well as of God's involvement in the destiny of the world of man. This is the deeper significance of our previous assertion that only the hiding God may be known to man. He is certainly not known by his essence. After all, God must hide his essence for the relationship to be possible; only by means of the relationship may he be known. He is known by the will with which he relates himself to finitude—a will that presupposes an act of self-abnegation. The relational attributes say nothing about the divine essence; rather, they describe the will of divine self-denial and self-limitation.

We may now be in a position to appreciate why nature, as we have maintained, offers no proof for God as its creator. Creation is not an act of divine expansion or the emanation of divine substance. On the contrary, it is divine self-control; it is the restraint of the divine essence by the divine will of self-limitation. Creation may, therefore, reflect the awesome traces of divine self-abnegation; it dare never, however, bear reliable testimony to the One and Absolute God. Unless we knew him, and knew him as the Creator, from the testimony of the encounter, we could not know him by means of a finite universe. God is neither in man nor in nature; there is no path that leads convincingly from nature to God.[15] The sense of awe that seizes us as we behold the majesty of nature need no more be ascribed to the perception of an ineffable divine Presence than the blind terror of nature's fury need be linked to the workings of some demonic demiurge.

Only he who knows of God the Creator from the encounter will recognize in nature God's creation. It is true that "The heavens declare the glory of God, and the firmament shows his handiwork";[16] but one must first know of him before one may behold his glory in his creation. It is not from gazing at the heavens that we become certain that they are God's work. Rather, it is that having learned to know God first, we realize that the heavens and the earth are his.

When I behold your heavens, the work of your fingers,
The moon and the stars, which you have established...[17]

CHAPTER EIGHT

Creation

We are in the fortunate position of being able to dispense with all the barren arguments to prove that the world was created with which the history of religious philosophy is cluttered. Not only is the religious idea of creation known from the encounter, but we have also seen that the religious interpretation of that idea excludes the possibility of any proof of a Creator on the basis of a deduction from nature. We may also recall what was said earlier about the need of religion for a hiding God: God hides in the encounter so that man may endure his presence. He hides in history, too, from the penetration of the intellect, so that man may retain his intellectual and spiritual freedom even while affirming and acknowledging God. It is therefore necessary that the works of God's hand not testify compellingly to their Maker. If they did, man would be forced to acknowledge him, and neither the encounter in "fellowship" nor the affirmation of faith in freedom would any longer be possible. Man would be a mere puppet of the Eternal.

Not only do we not have to offer any proof for creation beyond that which is made known to man in the encounter, but the religious position further requires that if such a proof were offered, it would be our duty to expose its fallacy. It is, however, still our responsibility to show that there is nothing in the rest of our knowledge that would render the acceptance of the idea of creation impossible. That is, we still have to prove that even if the creation idea is not provable, neither is its opposite; we must show that creation is not incredible.

David Hume reasoned logically that a cause may not be known by its effect if the assumed effect is unique in our experience. "It is only when two *species* of objects are found to be constantly conjoined that we can infer the one from the other [that is, the cause from the effect]; and were an effect presented, which was entirely singular, and could not be comprehended under any known *species*, I do not see that we could form any conjecture or inference at all concerning its cause."[1] The existence of the universe is just such a singular effect; we therefore cannot make any inferences concerning its cause. For this reason, creation cannot be proved by the argument that every effect must have a cause. At the same time, Hume's argument also establishes that if the coming into being of the cosmos is such a singular event that we cannot form "any conjecture or inference at all concerning its cause," then creation may be neither proved nor rejected. What Hume means is that creation would be an event outside all possible experience, and as such it could not be accepted as justified by "experience and observation." For the very same reason, however, it cannot be ruled out as impossible on the basis of "experience and observation."[2] Judgment will have to be suspended on the subject.

However, even though experience as such neither proves nor disproves creation, the question remains: Does it not have to be rejected because of the logical fallacy of the idea? Creation is understood to have taken place *ex nihilo*. But the very same logic that requires that every effect have a cause implies the premise that nothing will come out of nothing. Only on the strength of that premise are we compelled to search for a cause whenever an "effect" is observed.

This question has, it seems, been answered conclusively by Maimonides.[3] Following his argument, we might say that it is quite correct that in human experience, nothing happens *ex nihilo*; this fact, however, has no bearing whatsoever on the idea of creation. No one has ever asserted that *creatio ex nihilo* was an event within the realm of possible human experience. The idea of creation means that God created out of nothing a universe in which every effect must originate in something that was previously in existence. Out of nothing, God created a world in which nothing comes from nothing. One is therefore not justified in drawing conclusions from the observable order of things as to what might have been the "order" prior to creation in the timeless and spaceless state of divine "aloneness." The coming into being of the whole of the cosmos is an essentially different event from the coming into being of particulars within the framework of the already created whole. No deduction of any kind may be made from the one to the other. Therefore, notwithstanding the fact that in all of our experience, nothing comes out of nothing, the world itself may well be God's creation *ex nihilo*.[4]

Mainly because of the confusion of the concept of creation with that of causation, it was possible to imagine that scientific theories could ultimately replace the theory of creation. A useful illustration in this context concerns the theory of evolution.

When the evolutionary theory was first formulated in the nineteenth century, it raised a storm of indignation among the pious. It seemed to fly in the face of biblical teachings, and to this day it remains a popular "scientific" dogma that anyone who recognizes the validity of evolution has no need or use for creation.

We are not concerned here with the critique of the scientific validity of the evolutionary hypothesis as such. Our interest is, rather, limited to the connection that may exist between this theory and the idea of creation. Now, whatever evolution may explain, it does not explain the beginning. For the evolutionary principle to be effective, one must assume the existence of some material which is subject to its sway. Natural selection may perhaps bring about the survival of the fittest, but only if there has previously been in existence a whole display of variations from among which the fittest may be selected.[5] No matter how far back we pursue the rise of the variations over which natural selection exerts its control, we must still start somewhere with something that did not come into being as the result of evolution. Nothing will not evolve into anything.

Even in its most radical form, the evolutionary theory must begin with the premise that prior to all evolution, there was something in existence from which, as the result of the evolutionary principle, the rest followed. Once this is granted, however, the concept of creation retains its original significance. That there should be anything capable of evolutionary development requires no less interpretation than that there should be a cosmos, complete in its fullness and glory. Only Nothing is self-explanatory. The existence of Nothing is alone logical; indeed, it ought to be "expected." Being itself, of any kind, is the real surprise. In this respect, it makes no difference whether what exists is the smallest speck of something, to which the evolutionary theory may reduce the cosmos as its starting point, or the radiance of the innumerable galaxies in the universe. Indeed, the most illogical aspect of all our experience is that there should be anything and not nothing. The leap from Nothing to Something is the mystery of all mysteries. Compared with the crushing of the barrier that separates Nothing from Something, the path from something to all the riches of a cosmos is a mere bagatelle. But it is precisely with the crushing of this barrier that creation deals. To imagine that evolutionary theory could render creation superfluous is about as logical as to say that since the invention of the telescope, man no longer needs eyes.

What has been said about evolution applies equally to any other scientific theory that interprets the cosmic order. Whatever the theory, it must assume as fundamentally given something that cannot be reduced any further,[6] that cannot be scientifically explained—an illogical and irrational givenness, and yet the foundation of all order and the basis of all rational interpretation. How trivial is all scientific interpretation of the order in the universe, compared to the massive mystery of the "unnatural" givenness of being itself!

All scientific theory interprets the order in a cosmos that is most "unscientifically" given. Creation, on the other hand, relates the fundamental element of givenness to its source—to God, the Giver.

If we thus understand creation as the positing by God of the irreducible givenness of the universe, we may now take our analysis of the difference between causation and creation a step further. Once again, evolution may serve as our example. People might be inclined to say: Assuming the validity of evolutionary theory, how can one speak of the creation of the world by God? Creation of that something from which everything began, perhaps; but of the world? Surely once the primordial something was given there was no more need for a creator, since the rest followed as the result of evolutionary developments. Such notions, however, are a product of the confusion between creation and causation. For in fact, there is no contradiction between the idea that God created the world, on the one hand, and that the world evolved from the originally given Something, on the other.

We may illustrate this point by way of analogy. When Beethoven wrote the last note in his Ninth Symphony, the creation of that masterpiece was completed, even though the music itself had not been performed. The music never yet heard was, nevertheless, already created. Likewise, the orchestra which, after the work of the composer was done, "made" the music had nothing to do with its creation. Beethoven "made" no music, the orchestra "created" no symphony. Or consider, for instance, a structure like the Eiffel Tower in Paris. This masterpiece of engineering was created when Alexandre Gustave Eiffel, after conceiving the idea, made his calculations. It was in that phase that the tower was actually created, even though, apart from the blueprint, there was no sign of the tower anywhere on earth. If, owing to lack of money, shortage of material, or unavailability of adequate location, the tower had never been erected, Eiffel would still have been its creator. The builders of the tower themselves had nothing to do with its creation.

One might say, then, that Beethoven *created* the music, while the orchestra *caused* it to be; Eiffel *created* his tower, and the building contractors *caused* it to rise. Similarly, if on one terrible day all the trees on earth were cut down and not a single one remained in existence, it would not be necessary to *create* anew, but rather to *cause* them to grow again from whatever seeds or saplings might be left. The winter storms strip the trees of their leaves, and spring "makes" them grow again, but need not create them.

If we may be guided by these analogies—which, like all analogies, are inadequate—we might say that creation is the conceiving of an idea in a form that will render it capable of materialization. The envisioning of a tower that, when built, will not be able to stand is not an act of creation. The composition of a symphony that, through no shortcomings of any possible orchestra, is incapable of execution may be called an act of madness, but should not be confused with creation. After all, there was something "unreal" within the original concept.[7] Creation, on the other hand, is the formulation of an ideal concept, and its positing in a manner that will render its realization possible. Causation, however, is the actualization of the latent possibility established by a preceding act of creation. What we have called the crushing of the barrier between Nothing and Something is fully accomplished when the world comes into being as a potentiality. Compared to that primordial deed of creation, the transformation of the cosmos from potentiality into actuality is a very small matter indeed. The moment our logical starting point, Nothing, becomes impregnated with a potential universe, the world is created in all its ramifications; created, we say, even though not yet actualized.

Assuming now, for the sake of illustration, the validity of the evolutionary principle, we may say: By positing it as a potentiality, God indeed created the world as a whole; he also created the evolutionary principle,[8] which represents the mechanics of the actualization of the world after its creation. God is thus the creator of the world, including evolution. For the evolutionary principle is one of the causes that, within the scheme of creation, has been allotted the task of transforming elements of potentiality into actuality.

When we read in the Bible that "God said: 'Let there be light.' And there was light," it need not mean that God, like the chief engineer at the festive inauguration of a new power plant, threw the master switch to illuminate the universe. It is in fact quite conceivable that when God said, "Let there be light," darkness continued, feeling secure in its tenancy. Nothing at all may have happened; perhaps it remained as dark as before. Yet the dominion of darkness was nonetheless lost, for "there was light." Light had been created. It existed as the potentiality of light, waiting—perhaps—only for the cosmic engineer to install it in the universe. After light was created, it was up to some cause, some law of nature itself created, to turn the God-given potentiality of light into the actuality of suns, moons, and shining stars.

What has been said using the example of the evolutionary theory applies equally to any other interpretation of nature. All laws of nature, all patterns of order, or whatever else they may be called, can do no more than determine or describe the actualization of what is given in the act of creation. Science deals only with the techniques of actualization, which themselves are implanted in the cosmos by the givenness of creation. Therefore, whatever the theory of the cosmic technique may be, it will have no consequences for the idea of creation.

It is, of course, equally true that the idea of creation has nothing to say about the causal nexus of events in the post-creation phase of the cosmos.[9] Creation does not deal with the technique or method of actualization. It is thus surprising that for so many centuries people have read the story of the creation as if the Bible were a textbook on physics or natural history, or as if the story were meant to be a lecture on metaphysics or cosmology. In actuality, no theory of any kind is presented, but a number of statements of fact are made. God created; God spoke and there was; God made—all of this is so familiar to us that we hardly ever notice that not the slightest attempt is made to explain *how* he created, *how* he made, *how* anything came to be at his behest. Of course, our curiosity on this point could never have been pacified. Even if the process of creation had been communicated to us, we would still be like "the poor fool, as clever as ever before." The transcendental nature of the act of creation renders it inaccessible to human understanding.[10] The Bible tells us—of necessity—only that the cosmos came into being because God willed it to be. Obviously, a statement of this nature is not meant to offer any indication as to the behavior of the cosmos once it has been created.

Summing up our discussion, we may say that the primary significance of the biblical idea of creation is neither cosmological nor physical, nor even metaphysical; it is essentially religious.

The fact of creation, as conveyed in the Bible, reveals nothing about the manner in which the world was created, but it does establish the world's dependence on God. The cosmos came into being because God willed it. The fullest realization of this dependence, as discussed earlier, is gained in the encounter. It is, of course, not the act of creation itself with which man is confronted in the encounter. Facing the Presence in the encounter, man is overwhelmed with the certitude that God is the Creator, and that man is God's creature. This, again, explains man to himself. This is what man is—a creature of God; this is his essence. And knowing himself as part of the world, and acknowledging himself as God's creature, man comes to know that the world, too, is God's creation. It could not be otherwise.

The most far-reaching consequence of such a position is that it introduces the concept of value and purpose into the very core of reality. No doubt, a world created by divine desire and volition cannot be valueless. Nothing could be more incongruous than the pessimistic denigration of this world by the pious. The glory of a future life may be incomparable to that of the present one, but this life, too, is God's creation; as such it possesses the highest dignity imaginable, that of being willed by God. "And God saw everything that he had made, and, behold, it was very good."[11] These words do not mean that the development of the universe was, technically speaking, an ongoing concern; they represent a judgment of value, the affirmation of a quality desired by God.

Finally, creation, being an act of will, is motivated by a goal. God wanted this world for the sake of some purpose. Since it would be impossible for man to know of creation unless it were revealed to him in the encounter, he cannot expect to know of the divine purpose for man and the world unless it is made known to him through the initiative of God. Moreover, just as the notion of creation is conveyed only in its relatedness to man, without the fullness of its transcendental meaning—which, of necessity, remains forever hidden from him—so it must be with the divine purpose. If it is made known at all, it can only be in its relatedness to man; but certainly not in its absolute sense, not as the purpose desired by God for himself, as it were.

Man may never learn to discern the "objective" or absolute purpose set by God for his creation, but being convinced of the value of everything created by God, he cannot but have faith in a purpose—be it ever so hidden—in everything that exists.

CHAPTER NINE

Evil

When we encounter the world, one aspect of it immediately attracts our attention in a way that seems to contradict the religious concept of creation. In an earlier chapter we discussed the value of the universe as God's creation. However, when we turn to the world, it is not its value that stands out most convincingly. As the still unresolved problem of theodicy testifies, it is senseless waste and ignoble suffering that seem to dominate life within our ken.[1]

All the ingenuity spent on the solution of the problem of theodicy will not convince us that evil is not real, that undeserved suffering is so only in appearance, and that life does not abound in irrationality and meaningless destruction. No doubt, creation possesses breathtaking beauty. It is often awe-inspiring in its manifestations, exalting in its dignity, and enchanting in its sweetness. Yet it also contains elements of sordidness, misery, and indignity. And religion must have the courage to face this fact. We rightly reject the obdurate claims of religious thinkers through the ages to the effect that the universe is perfect, that only a perfect creation could have issued from a perfect Creator. Indeed, it seems no less than an act of impiety to maintain the perfection of creation in the face of all evidence to the contrary. It is surely the worst form of anthropomorphism to suggest that an omnipotent and omniscient God could be responsible only for an immaculate universe.[2] Such weavings of the human imagination are, of course, logically absurd: They suggest, guided by the insight of merely human understanding, what man would do if he were not man but God. But they are also impious, for such notions in fact prescribe that God must use his divine powers in conformity with human understanding. There is no getting away from it: We know of God from the encounter; from the same encounter we know him as the Creator; and we know also of the imperfections of the creation by our own experience. It is therefore an imperfect world that the perfect God desired to create.

In a way, such a conclusion coincides with what ought to be the logical expectations of the religious consciousness. God alone should be assumed to be perfect. Perfection is identical with God; it cannot exist outside him. But creation is, foremost, separation from the Creator. The world is apart from God; it is therefore, of necessity, imperfect. No one may presume to know why God desired to create at all, but it is not conceivable that creation could have been anything but imperfect. After all, a perfect creation would have extinguished itself by tumbling back into God. A faultless universe, devoid of evil, would not be distinguishable from the Creator; it would be one with him. In other words, it would not be a universe at all. Creation, as the "other" that confronts God, must forever remain imperfect. This, indeed, is the full significance of creation as an act of divine self-limitation.[3] It is through the act of divine self-denial that the world becomes finite and, as such, imperfect. It is an act of self-imposed "humility"—to use the talmudic term—to create the limited reality in which the world comes into being. Only an imperfect creation may exist as the nongod, beside and apart from God.

It would follow, then, that the world, as God's, has value; as creation, however, it is imperfect. Yet since imperfection is *essentially* attached to creation, it must itself be willed by the

Creator. God is the creator of the world's imperfection, which is inseparable from creation.

The prophet Isaiah seems to raise a similar idea when he discusses the concept of God's unity, when—as the mouthpiece of the divine word—he exclaims:

> I am the Eternal, and there is none else,
> Beside me there is no God...
> That they may know from the rising of the sun, and
>   from the west,
> That there is none beside me;
> I am the Eternal, and there is none else;
> I form the light and create darkness;
> I make peace and create evil...[4]

Undoubtedly, these words are intended to counter certain concepts that had their place in Persian mythology and later served as the foundation of Manichaeism and the dualistic gnosis. In view of the mixture of good and evil that prevails everywhere in the world, nothing could be easier than to see reality as the struggle between two antithetical principles, making the one responsible for everything good and reasonable, and the other for everything evil and dark. In the history of monotheistic religion, there have been many who, attempting to solve the problem of the existence of evil, went to the other extreme: Following Neo-Platonic ideas, they denied the existence of evil altogether.[5] This was, obviously, not the view of Isaiah. He had the courage to face the consequences that follow from the idea of the one Creator: God, as the source of all reality, is also the creator of darkness and evil.[6] In our own terminology, this amounts to saying that the element of imperfection is a necessary part of creation.

However, if this is correct, then the element of imperfection itself—as willed by the Creator—must have value; it must be necessary. Once this point is understood, the darkness and evil of which Isaiah speaks no longer have the same connotation as they would in a dualistic universe. Evil in Manichaeism is absolute and has its source in an independent principle. According to Judaism, however, there is no evil in the absolute sense. As with everything else that is part of creation, evil, too, has its source in the deed of the Creator; it has, therefore, a positive function. It is for this reason that Rabbi Akiva could exclaim: "Whatever the Merciful One does is for the good."[7] He did not mean to say that evil does not exist, but rather that it subserves a purpose that is good, because it is of God. In other words, there is evil, but no evil *principle*, in the universe.

I do not wish to try to offer here a solution to the problem of theodicy. In order to explain the ways of God, one must first be familiar with the divine purpose and know of all the consequences that will ultimately follow from the creation of an imperfect universe. But he who could penetrate as far as that would have to be omniscient himself. We may, however, be permitted to pursue, as far as possible, the logical implications of the position that I have outlined.

Indeed, it is not really difficult to point to some of the positive functions of the element of imperfection which inheres in creation. It is by now a commonplace that without evil, goodness would not be possible either. In a world without temptation, man could never be holy. In a society in which—owing to the perfection of life—war could "congenitally" never occur, peace is no appreciable ideal. Without the ever-present inclination towards selfishness and discord, there can be no ethical ideal and practice. Rationality needs the menace of irrationality in order to be effective and, indeed, in order to be.[8]

Strangely enough, this thought applies to the Absolute as well. The Absolute in its lonely infinitude is itself incapable of goodness or truth, of judgment or mercy, of forgiveness or love. God becomes the source of all value by positing himself as the challenge to all value: By creating the realm of imperfection, the non-god outside himself. Therein lies, perhaps, the ultimate meaning of the relational attributes. God is known only by the attributes of his relatedness to the world. He acquires these attributes in the act of divine self-denial by which he creates the world to which he then relates himself. Using once again the phraseology of Isaiah, we may say: Only by creating darkness can God form the light; only through the creation of evil can peace be made.[9]

It may also be argued that imperfection is the source of freedom in the world. After all, the absolutely faultless is unfree: A perfect being in a perfect world would forever live and act in accordance with its inherent law, from which no deviation would be conceivable. A universe of perfection would be as ruthlessly determined by its nobility as the most rigorously mechanistic one is held in chains by the inexorable sequence of cause and effect. The imperfection of creation is the incompleteness of an order, the looseness in a law, the realm of the unforeseen; it is the source of surprise and spontaneity. It is freedom's only chance. Imperfection represents the measure of freedom from the compelling discipline of complete order; it is the sphere of the contingent in the universe. Moreover, in the realm of consciousness, imperfection alone makes decisions possible. The element of imperfection, therefore, not only renders a system of values meaningful by positing its "adversary," as it were, to challenge it; but by allowing for spontaneity and freedom, it also establishes the basis of all conscious behavior as an act of responsible choice.

Imperfection, as the source of need in the world, is the challenge for man; as the source of freedom, it is man's only opportunity to address the challenge, with whatever success he may attain. Since man, without the challenge and the freedom of meeting it through responsible action, would not be human, we might as well say that, to the extent to which we are able to attach sense and dignity to human existence, man is of necessity linked to imperfection. He who desires man in all his human finitude and potential glory must also desire the imperfections of man's cosmic condition.[10]

In a perfect world there would be no challenge and no choice, no decision and no responsibility. It would perhaps be some ideal form of reality, of which we cannot form the slightest notion. As already indicated, however, both the perfect "man" and the perfect "world" would, in their metaphysical significance, coalesce in the Absolute. He who asks for a perfect creation really asks for the Neo-Platonic "Alone" and the elimination of creation.

All this seems to indicate that God, in creating the universe, has delegated a measure of responsibility for its own history to creation. We find ourselves not in a universe of puppets, dangling from the strings of the Almighty and obeying every one of his commands, but instead in a universe in which freedom makes the deed possible. No doubt, God took a risk with creation by granting it consciousness and free decision. Such freedom may be misused at any time, or it would not deserve its name. Yet there is reason to assume that the risk is a calculated one. The possibility of failure must forever remain in this world; otherwise freedom, choice, and responsibility would not be meant seriously. On the other hand, notwithstanding failure, creation as such cannot fail; the ultimate responsibility of the Creator for his work is itself the guarantee of final success. There must be safeguards against the threat from creation's imperfections; the extent of freedom is limited by the law. Failure is always a possibility, but it can never be fatal to the purpose of the Creator.

In looking for a suitable illustration of this point, one is reminded of the leaps of electrons from orbit to orbit within the atom. Thus far, scientific theory has not been able to explain the sudden appearance of the electron in one orbit at one time and in another at a different one. The electron seems to make its leaps spontaneously, as if it enjoyed the freedom to jump the way it pleases. However, the orbits themselves between which the leaps take place are well defined by the inevitability of a law. Thus, a degree of spontaneity appears to obtain within a predetermined structure. This may be a useful simile for what we have in mind. The freedom that has been implanted in creation is real; but the area to which it is applicable is circumscribed.[11] There are orbits of free decision and behavior within the law of God's purpose for creation. There may be failure in the orbits of the "free" leaps, but this failure does not have sufficient destructive power to cause the encompassing structure of divine law and intention to collapse.

Summing up our discussion, we may say that the work of creation is never complete. An imperfect world has meaning for man in its very imperfection. The universe is not necessarily all good; but, thanks to the element of spontaneity in it, it is forever capable of improvement. The possibility of improvement, however, is also a perpetual reminder of the threat of further degradation. This is the precondition of human responsibility in encountering the world. The "works of the beginning" never end because imperfection is forever a part of the world. The realm that it occupies may be increased or reduced, and therein lies the danger as well as the promise of freedom.

The attitude resulting from such a position may well be called a philosophy of critical optimism. There is imperfection everywhere, but in everything that exists there is value as well. However, the full worth of reality is found not in its actual, but in its potential, value. God's creation is good because it is capable of goodness. But independent of all personal experience with the obstinacy of imperfection, and regardless of the outcome of man's struggle with it, there is God, the Creator; and God will not be defeated.

II

ENCOUNTERING
THE WORLD

CHAPTER TEN

The Problem of Ethics

The prophetic encounter with God is of such radical impact that, in principle at least, it fully determines the nature of man's encounter with the "other"—that is, with God's creation. All encounters in this world are meetings of needs set in a context of value. The needs have their origin in the essential imperfection of creation; the value, in the act of creation. In the previous chapter we noted that value without need, giving us perfection, would extinguish both man and his world. Yet it is also the case that need without value would render all endeavor and striving unworthy of man. Only in response to the need that is at the heart of all meaning and value does man fulfill his destiny.

The paradigm of all encounters is man's encounter with God. God meets the other with concern and care. The manner of God's involvement in the world is the eternal example for meeting the other. Nothing that man may meet within this world can be as strange to him as he himself is to God. Yet God elevates man to "fellowship" with himself. Meeting the other, in the image of the paradigm of all encounters, is an act of creative fellowship through caring involvement. It is the essence of the religious way of life. It is the concept of *imitatio dei*, which has been introduced into Western thought by Plato,[1] and which the rabbis expressed in the following fashion in the Talmud:

> In the Bible it is written: "You shall walk after the Eternal
> your God."[2] But is it possible for man to walk after the
> Presence? Is it not written: "For the Eternal your God is a
> consuming fire"?[3] Rather, the meaning is: Follow him by
> imitating his dispositions. As he clothes the naked... so
> should you clothe the naked. As he visits the sick... so
> should you visit the sick...[4]

The "dispositions" are, of course, the relational attributes. Their
ultimate significance is that they provide the original pattern for
all relationship on earth.

Long before the Talmud and Plato, the idea found its classical expression in the words of the prophet Jeremiah, when he
proclaimed:

> Thus says the Eternal:
> Let not the wise man glory in his wisdom,
> Neither let the mighty man glory in his might,
> Let not the rich man glory in his riches;
> But let him that glories glory in this,
> That he understands, and knows me,
> That I am the Eternal, who exercises mercy,
> Justice, and righteousness on earth;
> For in these things I delight,
> Says the Eternal.[5]

The knowledge of God surpasses all other possessions. Signifi-
cantly, the prophet does not imply by it metaphysical meditation on the divine essence. God may be known only by his
relational attributes—by the nature of his involvement in creation, by the fact that he exercises "mercy, justice, and righteousness on earth."[6] Most important, however, is the concluding phrase: "For in these things I delight, says the Eternal."
That God relates to the world because he delights "in these

things" establishes the *imitatio dei* as the divine law for man. Because "these things" are desired by God, the relational attributes become the example to follow. The encounter reveals not only God's concern, but also what he desires of man. The relational attributes are God's law for man. God, whose essence is hidden and who reveals himself by involvement with his creation, making manifest "these things" in which he delights, is of necessity revealed as the Lawgiver. The delight of the Eternal is his law for man. Since all revelation is divine involvement with men, and since all involvement is affirmation of the things God desires, revelation and law are inseparable. The encounter at Sinai revealed God as well as his law to Israel.

We may also express the idea as follows: As religion is inconceivable without revelation, neither is it possible without the law of God. God's involvement in the world and his law for the world are one. The law is the bond that preserves the relationship of divine concern beyond the fundamental religious experience of the encounter itself. The encounter passes quickly, but the law of the Eternal remains forever. As the crystallization of what God desires of man, the law is the guarantee of God's continued interest in man. As long as God's law stands, he too remains involved in the destiny of man. When the mystery of the encounter has faded away, God is still related to man by means of his law. When the precious moment in which man is granted the certitude of the Presence has sunk into the darkness of the past, the "fellowship" with God may still be maintained by doing the will of God. The law is the avenue of contact beyond the point of encounter.

The essence of the law is the same as that of the encounter itself: It is an expression of God's continued concern with man. That God commands man is the proof that he considers man. The law represents the highest affirmation of man, as well as his crowning dignity. By giving man the law, his Maker declares: I do care how he lives and what he does with his life. Charging

him with the law, God testifies, as it were, that man is man
enough to live under the law. The law is the sign that God has
a measure of confidence in man. The command of God implies
the encouragement: I order you because I know you can do it.[7]
For who should know the nature of man better than his Maker?
The law, being willed by God, is an indication that man—by
fulfilling it—will reach the purpose contemplated for him by
the Creator.

Thus, the law itself is a manifestation of God's love.[8] And so
the rabbis taught in the Talmud: "Beloved are Israel, for the
Holy One surrounded them with commandments."[9] Being fully
aware of the implication of the law as God's concern for man,
Judaism—far from considering it a burden—recognized in it an
"object of desire"[10] revealed to the children of Israel. And so
the psalmist was able to sing:

> The law of the Eternal is perfect, restoring the soul;
> The testimony of the Eternal is sure, making wise
>   the simple.
> The precepts of the Eternal are right, rejoicing the heart;
> The commandment of the Eternal is pure, enlightening
>   the eyes.
> The fear of the Eternal is clean, enduring forever;
> The ordinances of the Eternal are true, they are righteous
>   all together.
> More to be desired are they than gold, than much fine gold;
> Sweeter also than honey and the honeycomb.[11]

What is the purpose of the law? In asking the question, it is
clear we are now walking on dangerous ground. Nor is it our
ambition to try and fathom the intentions of the Lawgiver. It is
enough for the believer to know he is to do the will of God.
He rejoices in the thought that, by obeying the command of

God, he may relate to his Maker and walk "with him" or "before him."[12] He is elated by the thought of the law as the lasting testimony of God's concern with his welfare. When asking about the purpose of the law, then, we ought to consider those aspects which seem significant in the context of our human condition and its problems.

The interpretation presented earlier emphasizes the ethical significance of the law of God. This was borne out by the quotation from Jeremiah. The relational attributes as a code for human behavior declare: When meeting the world outside, you do it by relating yourself to it, by establishing fellowship with it through caring involvement. This is the essence of the imitation of God, and it invests the law with an ethical purpose. This does not mean that the law is identical with ethics. The law has meaning on many levels of human existence, and only after analyzing them separately can we grasp its various implications for man. Undoubtedly, the law has meaning on the ethical level. It is the ethical relevance of the law that we shall address first.

Traditionally the laws of Judaism are divided into two main groups: One contains the laws ordering relationships between man and his fellow; the other, those of a purely ritual nature, as between man and God. At the same time, as is well known, the law of God in the system of Judaism is extremely ramified: It embraces the entire life of the Jew. Man in time and in space, man in society and man in the world, are the subjects of the law. The rhythm of the day and of the week, of the year and of the years, is determined by numerous regulations concerning times of prayer and of rest, times set aside for holiday observances. The law also prescribes one's dealings with the world of things about us by the many rules about foods to eat and not to eat, clothing to wear and not to wear. The pursuit of agriculture, the building of a home, have their respective observances. And, needless to say, the same is true of man's intercourse with his fellow man in society or in the family, in the state and among the nations. All are circumscribed by the law. Every important event in the life of the Jew is brought under the dominion of the law. There seems to be no niche or nook into which the law has not penetrated. The law is present all the time and everywhere. The Jew is indeed surrounded by *mitzvot* on all sides.

Now, the ethical significance of the laws affecting human relationships can be readily acknowledged. The laws of the second group, however, the purely ritual part, present a serious problem of interpretation. One may accept the need for some basic ritual practices and yet be nonplused by the elaborate system of Jewish ritual laws. What is the purpose of the numerous rules and regulations that seem to suggest a purely mechanical practice, without any spiritual significance? In the *Shulhan Aruch* it is even prescribed in what order a person should get dressed in the morning.[13] Yet the picture is in fact far more complicated. On the one hand, as we shall see, nothing could be further from the truth than to claim that the "ritual" laws have no ethical function. On the other, the ethical code of the law regarding man and his fellow is not as free of problems as would seem at first glance. So the necessity for further inquiry is not eliminated even if one acknowledges only the ethical principles of the law as being spiritually meaningful.

The idea of a revealed law, even if limited to the rationally understandable realm of ethics, presented quite a problem in the history of religious philosophy. At various times, religious thinkers inquired into the essence of a divine law. They wished to know in what its validity consisted. Was it valid because it conformed to reason or because it was willed by God? Already in early Islamic philosophy, two schools of thought grappled with the problem.[14] There were the "freethinkers" who maintained that the good must be inherently recognizable as such. Consequently, the intellect alone is the judge of its validity. The law is revealed by God because it has validity of its own, but it is not valid because it is revealed. The "fundamentalists," on the other hand, felt that if reason alone were to judge the validity of the law, this would make the event of its revelation superfluous. They, therefore, held that outside the will of God there was neither good nor evil. The good was good because it was commanded; and had God commanded its opposite, then what is now known as evil would have become good. This solution is, of course, far from convincing. It is difficult to accept the idea that God could have elevated what is now called evil to the dignity of the good in a divine code. Yet it is also true that if the validity of the law were to depend on the arbitration of the intellect, the paramount importance of the revelation of the law would be abolished.

These discussions left their mark on the development of Jewish philosophy. Saadia Gaon, influenced by the Islamic schools, divided the laws of the Tora into rational and revelational laws. Rational laws are those which may be recognized by reason; they were revealed so that mankind might enjoy their benefit before they could be discovered through the process of intellectual growth. The revelational laws are those on which reason passes no judgment. They were given by God in order to increase man's reward for obeying the divine will.[15] Saadia's solution is, of course, merely a compromise. Even regarding the "revelational" laws, it is hardly possible to say that they have no value of their own, and that their entire significance lies in that they, having been ordered by God, may render man worthy of reward or mark him for punishment, as the case may be.

The same controversy flared up again several centuries later between Thomas Aquinas and John Duns Scotus.[16] Aquinas, following in the footsteps of the Islamic "freethinkers," taught the rationality of the good, which might be known by the "natural light." Duns Scotus, on the other hand, in line with the Islamic "fundamentalists," affirmed the complete dependence of the determination of good and evil on the ground-less will of God.

From the religious point of view, we seem to be left with an insoluble dilemma. The validity of the law must be rooted either in reason or in revelation. But if the law has intellectual validity, what need is there for revelation; and if the law is not acceptable to reason, what use revelation?

In the great centuries of the European Enlightenment, phi-losophy decided against revelation. In the name of natural reli-gion, deism made itself independent of revelation, declaring the light of reason to be the only source of authority for the law. Immanuel Kant, for example, proudly proclaimed that "the true and only religion contained only such laws... of whose absolute logical validity we may become aware ourselves... [and] which we therefore acknowledge as revealed by pure reason."[17]

This bold cutting of the Gordian knot was, of course, no solution to the religious problem. The "true and only religion" whose laws are "revealed by pure reason" may be something noble; to call it religion, however, is justified only if we assume that everything true and noble is religion. This, however, is a compliment which religion, in loyalty to its essence, must refuse to accept.

It would seem, then, that not even the category of laws concerning man's relation to his fellow is free of problems. It is not easy to say which is the less perturbing difficulty: The question of what need there is for revelation, if the laws are to be accepted on the basis of their rationality; or our all-encompassing ritual code, which seems difficult to associate with any spiritual significance.

Before attempting to answer these difficulties confronting the idea of the law of God in Judaism, two basic problems of ethical theory, usually overlooked, must first be addressed. One is the question of the source of ethical obligation; the other is the examination of human behavior in the light of that obligation.

As to obligation, it is not enough to know the rational essence of the good and the right; one must also understand why it is imperative to adhere to the good and the right. The two are far from being identical.[18] And when we consider human behavior in the light of ethical obligation, the problem of all problems is, of course, how to induce man to act effectively in accordance with his obligation.

None of the extant theories of ethics are able to show that ethical obligation has its source in the essence of the good itself. Let us assume, for example, that hedonism is a logically valid theory. What law is there in reason to forbid a person to behave unreasonably and to act contrary to the pleasure principle? Reason may, of course, describe the consequences of such "foolish" action—but what if one does not care about the consequences? Or consider utilitarianism. Let it be granted that the greatest happiness of the greatest number is indeed the essence of goodness. How can it be proved that one ought to care about it, and that one should be morally condemned if one does not? It is not different with intuitive ethics either. Man may have some innate concepts of good and evil; he may even be able to entertain an intuitive appreciation that he ought to act in accordance with the standards of such an inborn ethical code. But since he is capable of disobeying his moral "instinct," what is there in the intellectual grasp of those intuitive ideas that will obligate him to obey?

Perhaps the most interesting illustration of this point is provided by Kant's categorical imperative. At best, Kant has shown that to act so that the maxims of our will may at all times serve as the principles of a general law is indeed an *a priori* requirement of "pure, practical reason." However, he overlooked the most important thing: To prove that man is *obligated* to act in accordance with this famous "factum" of reason. If Kant is right, one might say that an action which does not conform to his categorical imperative is not dutiful, as the term must be understood by practical reason. But he has certainly not established that it is man's duty to act dutifully in this sense. The categorical imperative might have been fully validated logically; it is unfortunate that it is neither categorical nor imperative.

Our second problem is even more fateful for human progress than the first. Assuming the obligatory character of an ethical code, whatever the source of obligation, how is mankind to be induced to act accordingly? Obviously, this is a question which ought to be of fundamental concern to all ethics. The finest rules of human conduct are of little worth unless people follow them. It is one of the recurring subjects of the dialogues of Plato: Is goodness teachable, and how should it be taught?[19]

The Socratic-Platonic answer to the inquiry is well known. The highest form of goodness is a kind of intellectual grasp of the supreme idea of being, and its contemplation. Goodness is therefore knowledge itself and, like all knowledge, it is teachable. This leads to the theory of "involuntary evil." All evildoing is the result of some miscalculation. Moral evil is the cause of the greatest unhappiness. Therefore, says Plato, "let us remember that the unjust man is not unjust of his own free will. For no man of his own free will would choose to possess the greatest of evils."[20] Moral turpitude is always due to ignorance and is involuntary. The entire history of humanism to our own day breathes the same spirit of intellectualism in ethical conduct. Education is the panacea for all problems of ethics. What people need is enlightenment. Give them schools, teach the human race, and all will be well.

Within the realm of Western thought,[21] one may see in Christianity the extreme opposite of the Socratic teaching. From the Christian point of view, it is futile to expect to teach goodness effectively. As the result of the Fall, man is so constituted that he is incapable of goodness by his own exertion. Man would indeed be lost were it not for God, who, like a true *deus ex machina*, saves him by the miracle of grace. Christianity too seems to have a theory of "involuntary evil." Here evil is, of course, not due to ignorance; yet it ought to be known as involuntary, since it is due to a corruptness of human nature itself, which cannot be mastered by natural means. Man can only be saved; he cannot improve.

Between the Socratic and the Christian traditions we may place, in this context, Marxian and various forms of evolutionary ethics. Dialectical materialism appears to be in one respect even more optimistic in its outlook than Socratic Platonism. According to it, there is hardly any need to teach goodness. Nor would it be of much use; ideas in themselves are powerless. The only determining factors are the material conditions of human existence. Organize them so that they serve the well-being of all men, and all will be well with mankind. Now, the optimism of Socrates at least has its logical justification in the light of the Socratic premise. There, the idea of the supreme good is ontological; it is the source of all reality as well as of all goodness. On this basis, the real and the good are of the same origin and essence. The good is also the cause of all order in the universe.[22] What *is* ought to be. Reality is on the side of the good. It may, of course, not be so at all; but, at least, this follows from the premises of the teaching. However, if one denies the reality of the realm of ideas altogether and considers everything dependent on a strict materialistic determinism, the expectation that any kind of a social order would solve the problems of men is a form of dogmatic optimism for which there is no justification at all, either in theory or in experience. The assumption that material satisfaction leads to noble deeds presupposes a blind confidence in the essential goodness of a human nature which only occasionally becomes perverted by hunger and cold. A dogmatic idealism is implied, ill-befitting a materialistic philosophy.

Nor is much gained by wedding materialism to what has been called evolutionary ethics. We need not here enter into a discussion of the many fallacies of such an ethics. Assuming that it does exist, its basic principle seems to be another categorical imperative, which might be formulated in this way: In all your actions follow the direction of evolution.[23] We take it that, on the basis of such a theory, "adaptive function" is also responsible for the "conscious purposes" of an ethical code. Acting in accordance with such a code, one would *eo ipso* follow the direction of evolution. One would exercise mercy, justice, and righteousness for evolutionary reasons.

Now, whether or not evolution explains the emergence of such terms, it is far from being an answer to our question: How does evolution induce man to follow its "direction"? By having brought about the emergence of "conscious purposes," it has also evolved consciousness. As a result of all this, man may follow the "direction" and be good or refuse to follow it and be bad. Assuming, again, that the evolutionary direction does lead to the ethically good, judging by experience it would seem that the human race, having evolved to the level of consciousness, refuses *en masse* to follow evolution. The vital question of ethical practice—how is goodness to be taught so that it becomes effective in human conduct—remains unanswered.

Of course, materialistic evolution cannot borrow the solution of its problems from Christianity. But it may perhaps adopt the Socratic-humanistic answer, that goodness depends on knowledge, by claiming that the key to ethical action is the contemplation of the direction of the evolutionary process. But if such enlightenment will indeed lead to ethical action, then it is proved that intervention by consciousness in the evolutionary process is possible because it falls in the line of evolutionary direction. And since whatever follows that direction is assumed to be good, all successful purposeful action would have to be called good. The test of evolutionary ethics would be success.

Whatever survives is ethical. On such a basis, there is no need to pursue the discussion any further.

Henri Bergson, having distinguished between the rationality and the obligation of the good, also understood the gravity of the problem of human conduct. He differentiated between the lower, self-centered morality of the closed society, like the tribe, family, or nation, and the higher, universal morality of the open society of humanity. He rejected the Socratic-humanistic position that ethics may be acquired by any form of intellectual exercise and seemed to accept the Christian viewpoint in part, in that he too believed that human nature might not be relied upon for moral behavior. However, he let the *elan vital* perform the task which in Christianity was the function of divine grace. Moral action, according to Bergson, is not left to conscious behavior. The human personality is much too fickle to be entrusted with so important a responsibility. Therefore, the *elan vital* assures effective ethical conduct by compulsion. In the closed society it takes the form of social pressure, which establishes moral action as a habitual reaction, corresponding to what is known as instinct in the animal kingdom. In the open society, morality—which is communicated by the individual genius of saints and prophets who appear "like the creation of a new species"—exercises a more or less irresistible attraction.[24] Social pressure and the rise of the "social ego" are facts resulting from creative evolution. All morality, therefore, "be it pressure or aspiration, is in essence biological."[25] In other words, according to Bergson, too, man cannot help himself. He is in need of salvation; but the savior is the *elan vital* that redeems biologically.

Bergson's was a bold attempt to solve our problem. The *elan vital*, which unlike materialistic evolution does comprise the spiritual and purposeful, entrusts the effectiveness of ethical principles to the safekeeping of powerful biological forces which may not be thwarted. Unfortunately, the French thinker did not seem to realize that he had impaled himself on the horns of a dilemma. He saw clearly that the conscious acceptance of an ethical code did not guarantee its realization. He therefore called in a form of biological compulsion to assure the effectiveness of moral principles. But the moment ethical obligation becomes a form of compulsion, however ingeniously implanted in the workings of evolution, it ceases being ethical. As Bergson himself points out, ethical obligation presupposes freedom of action.[26] Man acts ethically when, choosing among alternatives, he decides to act in conformity with the ethical demand. Therefore, either there is morality in freedom, and where there is freedom there is also the threat of failure; or there is creative, evolutionary compulsion and no ethics. Thus the problem remains unsolved. In reality we find that—assuming that mercy, justice, and righteousness are indeed nature's own "end" for man, as Bergson would have it—man seems to command sufficient freedom to be able to reject these ends of nature, and makes ample use of his freedom to do so. The *elan vital* does not seem to have been very successful.

We are thus left with the Socratic and Christian answers to the question of how goodness may be acquired by man. Neither of them, however, is supported by experience. Man may have ample knowledge of the good, yet more often than not he will act against his better insight. Moreover, the conduct in history of nations and societies, of classes and castes, provides us with a record of inhumanity that reduces to irrelevance the most sadistic crimes of individuals. In this respect, there seems to be little difference between ages of greater or lesser enlightenment; except that, in times of greater intellectual advancement, as knowledge increases man grows in power proportionately and becomes correspondingly more dangerous. The evil done by the power that knowledge provides has always eclipsed the good done by the same power. Notwithstanding enlightenment, man seems to remain an essentially unethical being.

Historic experience inclines us toward the Christian view, of the corruptness of human nature. On the basis of our experience, it is much easier to make a case that man cannot learn goodness than one that supports the Socratic-humanist position. But while history provides ample material for a theory of the hopelessness of human nature, it shows no convincing signs of salvation through divine grace. Since the day when such an act of salvation is supposed to have taken place, the criminality of man has not receded, not even in the wide realms of Christendom. Jews especially do not have to wander far afield for proofs. For them it is enough to recall what has befallen them during almost two millennia of exile in the Christian countries. The fate of the Jews in Christian lands, which in our own day was brought to its logical climax in the extermination of six million Jews, is irrefutable evidence that to this day mankind has remained unredeemed. All claims to the contrary are swept away like chaff in a windstorm before the martyrdom that Israel suffered at Christian hands through the ages.

CHAPTER ELEVEN

Divine Law and Ethical Deed

The two problems of the revealed law of God, which were discussed in the second section of the previous chapter, are not unrelated to the two problems of ethics which concluded that chapter. In the next phase of our discussion, I hope to show that the divine law has its ethical significance in that it offers a solution to those ethical dilemmas from which ethics is unable to extricate itself by its own strength. What appeared to be the predicament of religion in its ethical context was mainly due to the fact that the two fundamental problems of ethics were not understood.

The misunderstanding of the function of reason has been the tragic mistake which the Western world inherited from the Greeks. According to Plato, the ideas have power as well as authority. The same may be said of the forms of Aristotle. With the Stoa, the laws of reason are identical with laws of nature. Reason institutes laws, and it is also the most effective principle of order. This idea was adopted almost unquestioningly by Western thought. Once it could be shown that an ethical principle was reasonable, the need to prove that it was also obligatory was hardly ever appreciated. It was taken for granted that the reasonable was also obligatory. Similarly, it was assumed that once the reasonableness of the good was understood, reason itself would cause man to act ethically. Reason was believed to have authority to command, as well as power to compel. Starting from such premises, it was of course not possible to appreciate the significance of a revealed law. Only against the backdrop of such an understanding of the function of reason could the problem of revelation that we have discussed arise. If reason were sufficient to command and to make a person obey, then indeed the question was justified: If the law is reasonable, what need for revelation; if it is not reasonable, what use revelation?

But reason as such may neither command nor induce action. Reason is the faculty of understanding, of recognition and interpretation, of analysis or synthesis. Reason may tell the difference between right and wrong; perhaps even the difference between good and evil. It cannot, however, provide the obligation for doing good and eschewing evil. The source of all obligation is a will, and the motivation of a will is a desire.[1] Reason knows no desire, though man may desire to be reasonable. What ought to be ought, perhaps, to be reasonable; however, it ought to be not *because* it is reasonable, but because someone wants the actualization of that which is reasonable. Reason may describe what is; it cannot prescribe what ought to be, except hypothetically. If we wish to reach a destination, reason may advise us how to get there; it cannot, however, tell us what destination to choose unless it is informed in advance what we desire to find at our destination.

All authority of reason is hypothetical. The very laws of logical processes possess only such hypothetical authority. If one desires to think logically, one must observe them. But there is nothing in the laws of logic to obligate man to logical thinking, should he prefer foolishness to wisdom. Or to use a previous example, Kant's categorical imperative is essentially hypothetical: The entire *Critique of Practical Reason* proves only that if one wishes the approval of pure, practical reason, one should respect the categorical imperative. It is always a desire, and not objective reason, which by setting a goal moves the will, and it is the will that issues the command. Not everything that is desired and willed is good; but the good does not become an obligation until it is desired and willed. The nature of the obligation depends, of course, on the will from which it emanates. The source of the obligation may be individual desire. A man may recognize something to be good. If he desires it, determining his course of action by his desire-motivated will, he becomes his own lawgiver. Or society may be the source of the law; desiring certain common objectives, it may safeguard them by legislation. The essence of justice may be described in terms of reason; its obligation must forever be based on a will. This, however, is tantamount to saying that all law derives its authority from some form of "revelation." The lawgiver must make his will known to establish the law. Let a law be ever so rational, if it has not been instituted as such by the will of the legislative authority, made manifest in one way or another, it is not obligatory; in short, it is no law.

We may now appreciate how misguided has been the controversy concerning revelation and the rationality of the revealed law through the ages.[2] The arguments between "freethinkers" and "fundamentalists," between enlightened deists and traditionally inclined theists, were never resolved. Nor could they have been resolved along the lines on which the discussion was conducted. Both schools of thought were right as well as wrong. The "freethinkers" were right in maintaining that a law that could not be subjected to the test of reason was worthless; they were wrong in assuming that justification in reason makes revelation even partially superfluous. The "fundamentalists" were right in insisting that a law not revealed by God could not be considered of divine origin; they were wrong in asserting that the quest for intellectual affirmation was immaterial. Their dilemma was due to the confusion between logical validity and ethical obligation. They did not realize that the *summum bonum* might be rational and yet not obligatory, unless it were willed by someone in authority to command. The law of God may indeed be "perfect"; however, it becomes his law because it is willed by him. Were the intellect to grasp, through the faculty of its "natural light," a divine truth, this would mean entertaining a divine concept in the mind of man. If man desired and determined to act in accordance with that insight, he would make a divine truth his law of conduct. The intellectual validity of the law would then be divine; the ethical obligation, however, would have its origin in the will of man. An eternal truth becomes the law of God when action in accordance with it is explicitly desired by God. It is the *will* of God that makes the good obligatory as the law of God. Just as religion itself cannot be based on logical proofs for the existence of God, but only on the experience of God's concern for man,[3] so too the law of God cannot be established on the logical validity of any system of ethics, but only on the manifest will of God. We know of the law of God, as we know of any other law, because it has been revealed to us by the lawgiver.[4]

From what has been said, it follows that the concept of the law of God does not exclude the possibility of a secular ethics. In view of the difference between the logical validity of a code and its source of obligation, a valid code of ethics can be based on the exercise of mercy, justice, and righteousness and be made obligatory because man or society "delights in these things." Human behavior according to such a code would be ethical, yet it would be independent from a divine law. The same ethical code may be desired by society or by God; the difference will lie in the nature of the obligation. The binding force of a code instituted by society or the state is relative; the force of the one willed by God is absolute. It is not, however, in the difference in the rigor of its application that the distinction between relative and absolute obligation is reflected. A secular society need not be less exacting in its demand for obedience to its laws than a community governed by a divine law. Mercy as well as justice are the things in which God delights. But a law instituted by a will of relative authority admits of compromise for the sake of expediency; the law of absolute authority will not be overruled by such considerations. All secular ethics lack the quality of absolute obligation. They are as changeable as the desires and the wills that institute them; the law of God alone is as eternal as his will. Secular ethics, derived as it must be from a relative will, is subjective; God alone is the source of objectivity for all value and all law. Relativistic ethics, serving the goal of subjective desire, is essentially utilitarian; the desire of God alone makes the object of the desire an end in itself.

It is not enough, of course, to be able to point to the source of the obligation of ethical principles. As already indicated, the task is to induce man to implant the demands of morality in human conduct. We have observed that the dismal record of human performance in this area testifies to man's most tragic failure in history. This failure, I have suggested, is due mainly to the belief that reason implies both authority and power. The foregoing discussion addressed the matter of authority; what remains is the question of reason's power.

Assuming that the mind possesses power of its own, the Socratic theory of "involuntary evil" is correct. If ideas indeed possess a vital potency, then once they are grasped and contemplated, they will—most certainly—determine the actions of man. On the basis of this assumption, goodness becomes teachable via the intellect. All one needs in order to act in accordance with ethical principles is their conscious realization. Reason will then cause man to obey. The truth, however, is that the mind is incapable of action of any kind. The spirit by itself, within the realm of human experience, is impotent. It has rightly been observed that the higher forms of being, as well as the higher categories of value, are by themselves the weaker ones as measured in material potency.[5] The realm of existence which is blind to the ideal of truth as well as to any concept of morality—that is, inorganic nature—represents also the most powerful concentration of material energy in our experience. The spirit itself is powerless; it may act only in union with the vital or "material" forces in the cosmos. No one has ever accomplished anything by merely contemplating an idea. All conscious action is the result of some form of cooperation between the mind and the body. Matter—whatever its ultimate secret—without the mind is inanity; mind without matter is, at best, noble impotence. Power by itself is purposeless; purpose on its own is powerless.[6] The material world can be saved from the idiocy of mere being by the direction it may receive from the spirit; the spirit can be redeemed from the prison of its impotence by the amount of cooperation that it may be able to derive from the material world. Meaning is realized in this world by the interpenetration of mind and matter. Matter must be informed by mind, and mind must be rendered potent by matter.[7] Without interpenetration of the two realms, reality would simply be a jungle of blind forces, entangled with one another and, perhaps, contemplated by some mind that rationalizes the impotence of the spirit into stoic serenity.

Nowhere is this more true than in the realm of ethics. The ethical deed represents the unity of mind and matter; it results from an intimate cooperation between the ethical intention and the human organism which "agrees" to be guided by it. Without a living body, there is for man no possibility of doing good. (Without a normally functioning brain, one cannot even *think* of goodness.) All ethical principles depend for their materialization on the vital, organic element, which is inseparable in this world from the human personality. In the ethical deed, the mind guides toward a desired goal, and the organic element provides the practical means of reaching it. The spirit of man may recognize the end of ethical aspirations intellectually; his physiological and biological inheritance, constituting the human body, is alone the instrument of ethical realization. Without the cooperation of the body, the mind will achieve nothing.

Only now are we able to appreciate the seriousness of man's ethical predicament. On the one hand, the mind of man, the custodian of all spiritual and ethical values, is by itself incapable of action; on the other, the life forces and all the sources of material energy, without whose instrumentality no ethical action is possible, are by their very essence indifferent to ethical or spiritual values. All forms of energy are indifferent to considerations of righteousness or mercy; all biological needs or desires are unaware of the existence of any moral code. The human body, the tool of individual moral conduct, is essentially amoral. Indeed, since the prototype of all ethical action is God's encountering the world with care and concern, one might even say that the instruments of ethical realization are not only basically amoral but, indeed, anti-moral. As in the divine prototype, care and concern for the other require self-limitation and even self-denial.[8] But all the inorganic concentrations of energy in the universe meet their environment with the full impact of their self-concern. All the organic needs in nature seek their own satisfaction exclusively. Physiologically and biologically, the organic nature of man strives to preserve its vitality and effectiveness in an essentially selfish way.

At the core of human existence is the source of man's ethical dilemma. Man, taking his place in the realm of the spirit as well as of matter, is committed to ethical action. He is obligated to meet the other, the non-self, in a relationship of caring involvement. But he can do this only through the instrumentality of a physical organism which is in essence under the sway of laws of self-centeredness. Man appears to have nothing with which to overcome the dualism of his being, except this nature of his, within which the two principles are alive and at cross-purposes with each other.

From the ethical point of view, Plato was right when he defined man as a soul using a body. He was wrong, however, in going on to say that knowledge would ensure that man would make the right use of his body.[9] Knowledge by itself is never the cause of action. Already Aristotle subjected the Socratic-Platonic view of the teachability of goodness to pertinent criticism. He pointed out that the mind, being calculative and speculative, "is never found producing without appetite."[10] It is true that Aristotle also says that "appetite alone is incompetent to account fully for movement." Often one appetite has to contend with another and, at times, we may even resist temptation and follow the advice of the "practical mind"; but only because the "practical mind" itself subserves an object of appetite.[11] Ethical practice must be motivated by an emotional urge, and its effectiveness depends on the outcome of conflicting emotions and desires.

Aristotle, in his criticism, was anticipating Spinoza, who many centuries after him proclaimed that the intellect as such was powerless against emotions. He maintained that our knowledge of good and evil is unable to restrain emotions which are in conflict with such understanding, unless our knowledge itself becomes an emotion or a desire for the good, more powerful than the opposing desires.[12] While this insight is valid independent of his system, it is regrettable that Spinoza's solution to the problem of making intellectual concepts emotionally effective makes sense only on the basis of his own premises. What we observe in actual experience is the fearful impotence of the mind to curb, let alone rule, emotions. Only emotions seem to be potent enough to control or master emotions. All this seems to lead us to the Marxist position. It was Karl Marx who asserted that ideas become potent when they capture the *imagination* of the masses. This, of course, means that ideas, in order to be powerful, must serve goals that are emotionally desired by a great many people.

The Marxist rebellion against Socratic-humanistic intellectualism was fully justified. It was right in affirming the impotence of the spirit, as such, in the realm of events and actions. It was wrong, however, in concluding from such "material" impotence the nonexistence of an independent realm of valid ideas and values, which ought to inform events and guide actions.

Bearing in mind the complex nature of the ethical dilemma, how then is effective ethical conduct possible? In the approach to this problem, what I have called Judaism's critical optimism manifests itself in another form.[13]

The law, itself an expression of God's care for and confidence in man, outlines the human share of responsibility in man's salvation. There is a great deal man can do and, therefore, ought to do in the cause of his own redemption. At the same time, the extent of the law, which leaves no part of life untouched, should be understood as an indication that Judaism does not accept the facile optimism of the Socratic-humanistic tradition that all man needs for the good life is the intellectual study of the essence of goodness. According to Judaism, man judged by his own nature is not as hopeless a creature as Christian theology would have it; neither is he as easily led to goodness as humanism imagines. There is, indeed, a great deal man is able to do for his own redemption, but much more is needed than the contemplation of the good.

It is to the problem of ethical practice, of how to induce man to live in accordance with an ethical code which he acknowledges intellectually or by faith, that the seemingly irrelevant elements in the system of Jewish law provide the solution.

The motivation of all action being a desire, the ethical deed requires an "appetite for goodness." Judaism assumes that such an inclination is indeed implanted in human nature. It is the good inclination (*yetzer hatov*), which—like its adversary the evil inclination (*yetzer hara*)—has its seat "in the heart."[14] It is an emotional force, a desire for the good.[15] It is present in all men, but—unfortunately—it is helpless in the conflict with the other, self-centered and self-regarding urges and needs of physical man.[16] It is therefore necessary to foster the emotional force of the desire for the good, to increase its intensity and its hold over the emotional pattern of the human personality. In order to achieve effective ethical conduct, not the mind alone, but, foremost, needs and appetites have to be educated; the seat of desire in human nature must be so influenced that emotional forces are willing to submit to the discipline required for moral action. This, however, is not enough. Beyond the education of needs and desires, it is also necessary to make the physical organism of the human body, the "tool" of all action, receptive to the emotionally accepted purposes of the spirit.

This is a twofold task, the accomplishment of which is pursued along two lines, converging on a common goal. One may increase the intensity of the desire for the good by sublimating some of the egocentric inclinations of human nature. But the sublimation of desires is brought about by inhibition.[17] Preventing the satisfaction of natural wishes, we erect emotional dams, creating reservoirs of emotional energy. The resources of such reservoirs may then be so channeled as to increase the emotional "charge" of the desire for the good, thus enabling it to seek its own satisfaction more potently. Within the system of Judaism, the purpose of the method of inhibition is achieved by such "ritual" laws as belong to the category of the negative commandments (*mitzvot lo ta'aseh*). "You shall not do any kind of work on the Sabbath day" has obviously an inhibitory function as well. The same is true of the numerous dietary laws and of many other "purely religious" injunctions. There is within Judaism a code of commandments which achieves the inhibition of some natural needs and desires.

However, beyond inhibition—which as we shall see leads to sublimation—the law proceeds to the task of "educating" the human body, the indispensable instrument of all action, for the ethical deed. But how does one educate the body? Since the days of antiquity, Western civilization has mistakenly believed that it is possible to convince the body by reasoning with it, by telling it what it may and may not do. And so it hoped in vain for effective ethical conduct through education. At its best, Western civilization was talking to the mind and never really reached the body.

The body is not accessible to logical reasoning. One can only teach it by making it do things. One does not learn to swim by reading books on swimming technique, nor does one become a painter by merely contemplating the styles of different schools. One learns to swim by swimming, to paint by painting, to act by acting. One learns how to do anything by doing it. This applies nowhere more strictly than in the realm of ethical action. The only way of educating the biophysical instrument of action is by making it perform. This task is fulfilled by the other group of "ritual laws," which has its place in the category of commandments of positive injunction (*mitzvot aseh*), prescribing certain religious performances.

However, it may look as if we were running around in a circle. Was not our original problem how to make the biophysical part of human nature submit to the commands of the spirit? Now we seem to be suggesting that the only way of doing it is by making it submit. We inhibit needs and desires, we make a reluctant body perform all kinds of "religious" duties. If, however, we can do that, why not come directly to the point and satisfy ourselves with prescribing the ethical deed alone?

The problem is not essentially different from the one we face when teaching any other distinctive form of behavior or action. One does not teach the act of warfare merely by lecturing to recruits. One learns how to wage war best by waging it. On the other hand, to wait until a martial conflict actually arises would be foolhardy; it may then be too late to learn. The solution to the problem is, of course, military training. In this way one teaches the art of war by warring, except that the process of learning takes place in a situation of unreality. The peacetime maneuvers of an army may be planned to be as close a replica of the conditions of real warfare as possible; yet such maneuvers do not take place in the situation of real war. This, of course, is right and proper. It is true that one can learn to act in a certain way only by performing the action which is required. However, while one is learning one ought to be able to make mistakes without serious consequences. Therefore, one teaches people to behave and to do by making them behave and do, but in a situation that is artificially created for the specific purposes of "training." To send an army of raw recruits into battle may be the most direct method of teaching the art of warfare. Those who survive will learn fast and thoroughly. But the direct method is obviously not the wisest; and the more powerful the enemy, the smaller the chances of victory. All training teaches behavior by making a person do what he is expected to do. It is always partly inhibitive and partly prescriptive. It can be successful because it adopts what we may call the "indirect" method of teaching conduct. One is taught to act in an artificial situation, as if one were acting in a real one. One may succeed in acquiring a skill or an art because there is always a "second chance." In the "as if" situation of training, mistakes are hardly ever fatal and, therefore, one may try and try again.

Similarly, the ethical significance of the two categories of "ritual" laws, which we have been discussing, consists in that they ready the biophysical organism, the only means of ethical conduct, for effective ethical action by setting up the classical training situation. Any one commandment of the Decalogue— "you shall not commit adultery" or "you shall not kill" or "you shall not covet"—is an ethical injunction directed to a real situation of conflict or temptation. In order to obey it, one must inhibit powerfully aroused passions. But one does not learn the art of self-control by merely reading the Bible. One learns it by actually controlling oneself in the face of a challenge. However, when the challenge actually arises in all seriousness, it may be too late to inhibit and to act ethically and effectively. To delay one's preparations for meeting the challenge until it actually presents itself would be the direct method, which usually leads to failure. The direct attack on the amoral and, perhaps, even anti-moral egocentricity of the physical organism is as unwise an undertaking as the sending of untrained recruits into the firing line. Emotions will be mastered only by stronger emotions. The dynamic charge of vital urges will be held in check by the more potent charge of opposing and no less vital desires. But, originally, the desire for the good, as one of the vital urges within human nature, is outnumbered by opposing forces.

The educational significance of the inhibitive as well as positively enjoining "ritual laws" is that they represent the *indirect* attack of Jewish intention on the essential self-centeredness of the biophysical element, the unwilling yet indispensable partner in the ethical life. Both the inhibitive and the prescriptive regulations of this code, from the point of view of ethical training, follow the indirect method. By referring to them as "ritual" laws, we express the idea that there is no logical reason for their being laws at all. There is, for instance, nothing in the real situation of man to suggest that it is harmful to partake of food that is forbidden by the dietary laws. It is the law itself that creates an artificial situation, as it were. It orders people to behave "as if" it mattered what type of food they consumed.

Or let us take another example, one which is not inhibitive but prescribes some form of action: The commandment of the daily wearing of phylacteries. Again, there seems to be nothing in the real situation of man to require such an exercise. It is the law itself which creates a situation in which the performance of this religious duty is treated as seriously as if something important depended on it. It is the typical "as if" training situation. Judged by the reality of the immediate situation, the soldier engaged in camouflage exercises, his helmet adorned with branches and leaves, not daring to move lest an enemy take a shot at him, when obviously there is no enemy, does a silly thing. Seemingly, he is engaged in an equally absurd task when he aims his rifle, loaded with make-believe bullets, at a make-believe target. Yet on such make-believe may indeed depend his very life, should the "as if" situation ever turn into a real conflict.

The training method of the "ritual laws" approaches the citadel of biophysical egocentricity indirectly: It never demands complete self-denial from it, as is exacted in the real situation of conflict and temptation. At no time, for example, does the observance of the dietary laws require complete denial of one's need for food, meaning the absolute suppression of "appetite." The inhibition is always partial and temporary.[18] Similarly, in those regulations that prescribe certain duties to be performed, what is demanded is of course not what the human organism, following the promptings of its own nature, would normally be inclined to do. Yet the submission exacted by the law is again only temporary and partial. To put on the phylacteries, to observe the three times of daily prayer, to pronounce a blessing before the enjoyment of the fruits of the earth—these require some submission, some discipline, some sacrifice. However, the self-regarding interests of vital needs and inclinations are not radically challenged. In submitting to the discipline of the "ritual laws," the egocentricity of man's organic nature is not directly assaulted. Because of the limited objective of the law in this

context, it is possible to achieve some success by making appetites and desires obey, by curbing some of their exclusive self-
seeking, and by causing the body of man to perform at the
bidding of a will whose desire does not have its place among
bodily desires and needs. The indirect method deals cunningly
with the "evil inclination."[19]

We may now say more exactly what is being accomplished
in the interest of ethical conduct by the observance of the
"ritual laws." The aim is to teach purely subjective emotions,
needs, and desires a new "awareness," one which is foreign to
the organic component of the human personality. It is the
awareness of the other, of an order of being as well as of meaning
different from that of organic egocentricity. The purpose of the
inhibitive rules is to practice saying "no" to self-centered demands; whereas the fulfillment of the positive commands is the
exercise of saying "yes" in consideration of an order different
from one's own. By such training, one breaks down the exclu-
siveness of man's organic selfishness. The obedience to the rules
and commands is itself an exercise in behavior that is not purely
self-regarding and orients a person toward an other. Submission
to the law becomes submission to an other; awareness of the
other means acknowledging and considering it.

We are dealing with the reactions of the human body. The
awareness of which we are speaking cannot, therefore, be
conscious. Physical awareness is instinctive or habitual. The
acknowledgment of an other must be made habitual in order
to be effective. This may be accomplished by a method of
training that is comprehensive and continuous. The religious
system of Judaism, which disciplines the Jew in every situation
all through life, establishes habitual patterns of physical reaction and conduct, which testify to an acute physical "awareness" of an order of reality that is not of the body. When, for
instance, a religious Jew feels nauseous when forbidden food is
placed before him, such a reaction is not natural; it is not in

keeping with the laws of his original physiology. The reaction shows the awareness of an outside will and law that the physiological element has somehow acquired.[20] In a sense, the nausea reflects the partial transformation of the natural desire for food, which has become retrained by the desire of the lawgiver. People who pray regularly and on all the occasions prescribed by religious law at times find that their minds have wandered far from the meaning of the prayer. Yet their lips—apparently guided unconsciously—continue to form the words automatically. Such, of course, is not the ideal form of prayer; at the same time, it is no small achievement to have taught the lips to "pray" on their own, without the conscious participation of the heart and mind. It shows that the human organism, from whose own nature hardly anything could be further removed than the wish to pray, has actually submitted to direction by the will to prayer. The physical element has become "aware" of that will in the same way in which it is "aware" of anything else, i.e., habitually; it has absorbed guidance from the intention to pray, and it respects its existence. Automatically "praying" lips may count for little in comparison with *kavana*, the directedness of the praying soul toward God in ecstatic submission; yet they too represent a form of submission of the organic self to the will to pray. In the Talmud is found the remark that we owe a debt of gratitude to the head because it bows, as prescribed when we reach the paragraph of *Modim* in our prayer, without waiting for the explicit order from our consciousness to do so. It bows mechanically, as it were, even when the mind has digressed from the contents of the prayer.[21]

No doubt, such behavior is not the most ideal approach to God. However, the value of a culture is expressed not in what people think consciously, but in what they do habitually. The civilization of the highest order is that which succeeds in teaching man's physical self to show, in its own "automatic" way, respectful submission to an order that is determined by the desires of the spirit and the longings of the soul.

Through the all-encompassing discipline of religious observances, the awareness of the other affects the habits of the entire physical element of the human being. The inhibitive regulations establish a pattern of behavior which disciplines the self-regarding impulses and, therefore, directs the "attention" of the unspent emotional energies toward an outlet by means of sublimation. At the same time, the prescriptive laws develop physical dispositions and skills to act at the behest of a will outside the physical realm. All this is pursued by the discipline practiced in the "as if" situation, by means of the "ritual laws."[22] But when the real situation of temptation, or the conflict of impulses and intention, arises in all seriousness, one has already practiced inhibition for the sake of an "other"; in innumerable previous situations, one has actually considered the other by making the body act as commanded by a will from outside the realm of organic self-centeredness. In the situation of serious challenge, one may therefore count on a measure of preparedness to obey instructions issuing from a higher order of values.

CHAPTER TWELVE

The Holy Deed

At this point the question may be asked: Assuming that the "indirect method" does indeed condition the vital drives and train the body for behavior that is not exclusively egocentric, what need is there for associating such an education with laws that emanate from God? Could such discipline not have been devised equally well by some human agency? Man has created many such systems of disciplinary training. The impressive history of military art in all ages is a case in point; the English public school system may be considered another; the art of yoga may also serve as a particularly convincing example. In all these cases, without any specific reference to God, success has been achieved in educating a new form of "awareness" and in establishing habitual patterns of behavior previously unknown.

Our question might be answered as follows: Since God desires of man that he practice mercy, justice, and righteousness, and since he desires this because he is concerned about his creation, it need not be contrary to good sense that he also prescribe a method that would help man in reaching the goal set for him by his Creator. Such an answer is problematic, however, because it limits the significance of the "ritual laws" to the function they perform in resolving the dilemma of effective ethical conduct. But the "ritual laws" are not merely the handmaid of ethics. Their meaning is far from exhausted by the "indirect method" with which they address the problems of successful moral action. Rather, their immediate significance is to be described in purely religious terms.

The "indirect method" helps in deciding the conflict within man in favor of the good; it serves as a bridge between the image of God imprinted on man and the material component of human existence. All this belongs in the realm of ethics. There is, however, another dualism—perhaps even more critical—that must be resolved, in the realm of religion. We have seen that the basic religious experience is one of relationship between God and man.[1] God cares for man and makes himself accessible to man. But the relationship, when it is established—either in the acute phase of the encounter or in the latent one of faith[2]— may occur only between the spiritual personality of man and the manifestation of the divine Presence. It would seem that the biophysical component of human nature is incapable of any relationship with the divine. The "organism" is not only amoral but fundamentally profane. This is the origin of the "religious" rejection of the body. Most higher religions are unable to make sense of the body. They see in it the throne of evil and suggest that man would be better off without it.

What the idealism of numerous religions and philosophies overlooks is that man without a body is as little to be considered human as man without a soul. Whatever the plight of the soul after death may be, in this world man is a composite being, consisting of mind and matter, of soul and body. That God made him that way means that he has to make sense of his life in the form in which he was granted life. Any rejection of the body is a rejection of man himself, of man as God created him for the tasks of this world.

If religion is relatedness to God, then the whole human being must be so related and not man as soul only, for as such he does not exist in this world. Man, soul and body, must enter into the relationship. This may actually happen in the prophetic encounter itself. There man is not at all in his own power; he is completely overwhelmed, as well as completely sustained. At the manifestation of the divine Presence, body and soul become one in their nothingness and, as one, are sustained in the elevating love of God. In the encounter itself, the dualism of human nature is overcome by the power as well as by the love of God. But in the post-encounter phase of religion, when the relationship is maintained by historic memories and the art of faith[3]— and this phase comprises all the life of most men and most of the life of all men—how is man's physical being to participate in the relationship? Is only the conscious element of the human personality to be related to the religious experience? Is only the soul to live in the divine Presence? If so, then man as man would be incapable of religion.

The task of relating the physical component of the human being to God can be accomplished only by a divine law. The body cannot meditate divine truth; it can only do or not do, behave one way or another. It may enter into the religious relationship only by means of its own nature—through action and behavior, undertaken in fulfillment of a divine command. It is true that the purely ethical function of the "ritual laws" might be achieved without their being divine commands; but their religious function cannot. On the religious plane, the indirect method of ethical concern becomes direct religious commitment. The training by the indirect method conditions the human organism for non-egocentric action; the origin of the law in the divine will, however, turns the non-egocentric conditioning into theocentric behavior. The "awareness" established is not directed merely toward some outside order, but toward a divine one. It is not just "an other" which the organic component of the human being senses, but the "Wholly Other" that is God. From the ethical standpoint, inhibiting some of the radically self-regarding impulses is a negative act; but in the religious context, by inhibiting one fulfills a divine command.

Not only does one learn to submit to an outside will; one obeys the will of God.

By obeying the command of God, the human organism itself becomes related to God; by *doing* the will of God, it is enabled to enter into relationship with the divine. The dietary laws, for instance, not only have the disciplinary significance of "educating" man's appetite; by obeying divine injunctions in one's eating habits, a basic human need enters into the religious situation. Or consider the traditional way of observing the Passover festival. Spiritually, one could commemorate the miracles that God wrought in Egypt by some form of intellectual exercise, such as thinking of the Exodus, remembering the events that led up to the liberation of our people, or contemplating the debt of gratitude we owe God for his intervention on behalf of Israel. All this is, of course, included in the traditional observance. But the physical element cannot participate in any form of spiritual celebration. The body may be induced to "remember" and to observe Passover only by our making it do things that have a bearing on the meaning of the festival; by refraining from all leavened bread, by partaking of the *matza*, by reclining at the Seder table. To cleave to God is, undoubtedly, a deeply religious concept, and one may have a pretty good idea how the soul may attempt to do it. But such cleaving will be of a spiritual nature. However, the body of man may learn how to cling to him only by performing some physical action symbolic of the spiritual meaning. The daily wearing of the phylacteries, for instance, may be considered such an action of "binding" the body, too, to God.

The religious significance of the "ritual laws" is that they create a material "awareness" of the divine Presence. As discussed in the previous chapter, this kind of awareness is not the same as that of the mind. It is not a conscious awareness; it is more akin to instinct. It must become a habit, to some extent subconscious, in order to assert itself in practice. Therefore, as seen earlier from the standpoint of ethical conduct, and now from the religious point of view as well, the system of the ritual laws must be all-embracing in order to develop the awareness of God as a secondary instinct, as it were, for man's physical being. The so-called ritual laws are the only way for the physical component in man to become oriented toward the divine; through them, the body too may cleave to God. By fulfilling the commandments of God, the body too may enter into the relationship that is the essence of religion.

The spiritual quality of both the worship and the service of God has been exalted too often. But such service applies only to one part of the human being; and as such, it underscores the religious impotence of the other. If the relationship to God is to be complete, it must engage man in his entirety. We can know nothing of the religion of a pure soul. Our task is to establish the religious reality of man. In the history of religious thought, a great deal of unjustified criticism has been heaped on the mechanical, ritual performances of religion. What is more important, the conscious worship of the mind or the quasi-automatic performances of the body? The question is meaning-less. The body cannot worship consciously, and the mind is incapable of serving by way of "ritual" practice. Since man is neither only soul nor only body, but both joined to each other, both these constituent elements must be related to God, each in a manner adequate to its own nature. On the level of the soul, the relationship is spiritual and conscious, but it cannot be expressed in action; on the level of the body, the relationship has to become "materialized" in action.

These two expressions of the religious life are not meant to exist parallel to each other as the religion of the soul and as that of the body. The *mitzva* is the union of the two. It is never only thought, nor is it a mere reflex movement of the body. In its ideal form, the *mitzva* is a deed; and, like all true deeds, it is of the spirit and of the body at the same time. In fulfilling a *mitzva*, the Jew consciously orients himself toward God; by doing the will of God, he knowingly places himself in rapport with the divine Being. But all this is the internal and invisible content of the *mitzva*; its external reality is constituted by the action of the body.[4] In fact, only because of the conscious element in the *mitzva* are the ritual laws able to establish the new bodily "awareness" as habitual orientation toward God. The conditioning of the body toward the will of God is the result of continuous conscious suggestion. Through the *mitzva*, man overcomes the dualism of his nature in the God-oriented deed. In the *mitzva* man is one; as a whole he relates himself to the one God.

The most revealing example in this connection is, perhaps, the case of prayer. No doubt, it is possible to pray "in one's heart," without words and without any movement of the body. One may pray in silent meditation. However, while such prayer may be appropriate for a being that is pure mind or soul, it is certainly not the adequate prayer for a being like man. The perfect prayer on earth is the one prayed not only by the soul of man but by the whole of the human being, body and soul. As the psalmist exclaims: "All my bones shall say: Eternal, who is like unto thee?"[5] Man's situation requires that his very bones should be capable of "prayer." But this is only possible if prayer too becomes a *mitzva*, unifying body and soul. Prayer, therefore, cannot be only silent meditation; it has to be a spoken word.[6] It has to be physical action, informed by intention. Physical prostration before God is no less essential for prayer than is spiritual concentration. The prayer of man should be human and not angelic.

The idea is magnificently formulated in the *Nishmat* hymn of the Sabbath morning service:

> Therefore, the limbs which you have apportioned in us, the spirit and the soul which you have breathed into our nostrils, and the tongue which you have placed in our mouths

shall all thank and bless, praise and glorify, extol and revere,
hallow and do homage to your name, our King.[7]

What is here said about prayer applies to religion in general. It
is comparatively easy to serve God as a spirit; the challenge is to
serve him in the wholeness of man's earth-bound, and yet soul-
indwelt, humanity. Immanuel Kant once wrote: "The true
[moral] service of God is... invisible, i.e., it is the service of the
heart, in spirit and in truth, and it may consist... only of intention."[8] This, indeed, is the noble formula for the historic bank-
ruptcy of all "natural," as well as "spiritual," religions. The
invisible service of God is the prerogative of invisible creatures.
When man adopts such service for himself, he makes the dualism of his nature itself a religion. He will expect *Gesinnung*
(sentiment) and noble intentions of the soul, and will readily
forgive the profanity of the body; he will have God "in his
heart" and some devil directing his actions. He will serve God
on the Sabbath and himself the rest of the week. He will
worship like some angelic being in the specified places of worship and follow his self-regarding impulses everywhere else.
And he will find such an arrangement in order. For should not
the true service of God be invisible? And is not the physical
organism—and together with it, all the material manifestations
of life—therefore incapable of religion?

Contrary to Kant, Judaism teaches that man's "true service
of God" must be human. It should be invisible, as man's soul is
invisible; and it should be visible, too, because man is visible. It
must be "service of the heart, in spirit and in truth" as well as
of the body. It must be service through the *mitzva*, the deed in
which man's spiritual and material nature have unified. It is a
much higher service than that of the spirit alone. It is the
religion of the whole man.[9]

The essence of such service has been beautifully expressed
by a latter-day rabbi, who said that of all those commandments

that are "between God and man," he loved most that of dwelling in the succah. In entering the succah, one steps into the *mitzva* with one's very boots on. This is, indeed, basic Judaism. It is comparatively easy to relate the spiritual to God; it is as easy as it is ineffective in history. The real task is to orient the whole world of man, matter and spirit, toward God.

Thus far, only continuous sacrifice has been demanded of man's material nature. The indirect method, as training for ethical conduct, inhibits natural impulses and undermines the self-centeredness of man's physical being. On the religious level, too, the creation of what we have called a physical "awareness" of the divine Presence is achieved at the cost of considerable physical self-denial. However, once the idea is accepted that man as a whole being is to relate himself to God, the self-denial of his material nature reaps its own reward. In the *mitzva*, which is realized by the union of the spiritual and material, the vital needs and functions of the physical component of man receive their affirmation. If they too are to participate in the relationship that is the religious life, then they too are wanted by their Maker; they too are acknowledged by God. The insistence that the oneness of man be achieved by overcoming the dualism of his nature implies that the material and organic have their own positive value. Far from being rejected, they are actually desired. In the attention given them, they are vindicated.

This vindication finds its expression, first of all, in the general acceptance of life as a basic value. The preservation of life is a fundamental religious commandment, which—with three exceptions—takes precedence over all other religious laws.[10] To preserve one's health and not expose oneself foolishly to danger is itself a divine command. Unlike Plato, Judaism does not look upon the body as "a prison of the soul."[11] It is, rather, essential and prerequisite to human existence. In view of the long history of idealistic misconceptions, it cannot be repeated often enough that the soul as such is not human. Man needs life, in the purely biological sense of the word, if he is to fulfill his divinely ordained destiny on earth. Life itself is God-given; it possesses meaning and worth in its material, organic manifestation.[12]

However, apart from the vindication of life as such, in the attempt to relate the whole of man to God, the particular needs, urges, and appetites of man's biophysical aspect find their affirmation as well. Again we may look to the example of the dietary laws. In fostering certain eating habits, these laws implicitly acknowledge the claims of a purely biological need and desire. The Jew who, in submission to God, satisfies his hunger by curbing the self-centeredness of an organic impulse has succeeded in serving God, even by the purely material activity of keeping his body alive. Even when eating, he lives in the presence of God.[13] "Blessed are you, Eternal our God, who brings forth bread from the earth," the blessing a Jew says before eating bread, is not only a form of divine service, but also encourages man's enjoyment of bread as God's creation.[14] The enjoyment itself, essentially biological, becomes oriented to God, because the blessing prepares for it spiritually. "He who sees handsome people and beautiful trees," the rabbis taught, "should say: Blessed be he who creates beautiful things."[15] By reciting the blessing, which at first intervenes between man and his enjoyment, man turns his sensual delight into an act of thanksgiving to God for his creation. In this way, earthly delight becomes justified through its relatedness to God.

Such affirmation of earthly needs and impulses is characteristic of the whole system of the law of Judaism. Sabbath and holidays are not observed "spiritually," nor should they be. Man is not a spirit. On the Sabbath, therefore, not only the soul should find peace, but the body too should rest. One celebrates the day not only by meditation and prayer, but also by wearing

Sabbath clothes and by enjoying the Sabbath meals. The Sabbath meal itself is a *mitzva*; it is divine service. Properly performed, it is service of a far higher quality than that of prayer and meditation alone; it is the service of the whole man. Body and spirit celebrate the Sabbath in communion. The Jew who keeps the Sabbath may say that the material enjoyments of the day enhance his spiritual elation, and that his spiritual elation renders the material enjoyments more gratifying. In the unifying act of the *mitzva*, the Sabbath acts as a "spice" to the palate, elevating the spirit of man.[16]

The biological functions, under the discipline of the law, fulfill the purpose desired by the law. The prohibitions of the law themselves imply a proper direction for these functions. Sexual morality, for instance, through its many inhibitive rules, prescribes the positive function of sexuality. As a result, we find that within Judaism it would be inconceivable to regard marriage as a "lesser evil," which, as a compromise in a hopeless situation, may be allowed to the lesser breed of men. Nor is marriage merely permitted, but rather an important religious obligation. According to the Bible, after the creation of man, God blessed him with the words "Be fruitful, and multiply, and replenish the earth."[17] The words of Isaiah that God created the earth "not a waste; he formed it to be inhabited"[18] were understood by the teachers of the Talmud to mean that man's duty is to ensure that the earth not become a waste, and that it remain inhabited by people.[19] Of the bond between husband and wife, the rabbis had the boldness to say: "If husband and wife merit it, the divine Presence dwells in their union."[20]

One should serve God with one's entire being. But one can do this only if the self-centeredness of man's vitality is curbed and his organic reality conditioned for the awareness of the divine. Through the education of man's physical component in the will of God by means of an all-embracing system of religious observance, the biological functions themselves become dedicated; man's nature becomes purposefully directed and may now fulfill itself and yet serve God. Only here do we reach the most intimate interpenetration between mind and matter, the closest union between spirit and body, between the needs of the creature and the purpose of the Creator. It is possible for man to satisfy all his needs in doing the will of God.[21] It is here that man's dual nature is brought to harmony. It is the vindication of matter through its union with the spirit and its association with a divine purpose.

This vindication of matter is itself an essentially religious task; it is part of the basic religious obligation which we have described as *imitatio dei*.[22] The original religious experience is man's encounter with the divine. In this encounter we discern God's care and concern for man. From this follows the religious duty to meet the "other" as God meets man, with care and concern. Now, one of the most elementary meetings with an "other" is the confrontation between man's conscious self and his material condition. The body does not meet the spirit, but the spirit does meet the body. Whatever the distance between the two, it is as nothing when compared to the abyss that originally separates man from God. Notwithstanding God's nature as "Wholly Other," the love and pity of God for man allows the encounter to take place. How much more should the spirit of man, in imitation of God, meet the body with pity and care.[23] The rejection of man's physical nature is an act of irreligion; it is conceit of the spirit and irreverence toward God's creation. While such rejection may occasionally be acclaimed as the unnatural triumph of rare individuals, in the history of man it always leads to the undoing of the spirit by the vengeance of the neglected drives of human nature.[24]

For the soul of man to meet the body of man, it should become the helpmate of the body, directing its impulses toward an acknowledged goal that is acceptable to those needs as well; it should work for their dedication in such a way that they may find fulfillment and at the same time perform the bidding of God. When matter becomes vindicated in this way, and the harmonization of human nature is thus accomplished, the soul of man has made its insights available for the guidance of the body, and the body of man has lent its vital effectiveness to the aspirations of the soul. Through their union in the *mitzva*, the great transformation takes place: The spirit becomes "material-ized" and, therefore, effective; the body is "spiritualized" and, thus, oriented towards the divine. This is holiness.[25]

The spirit is never holy by itself; there are no holy ideals or holy intentions. Holiness is only possible where the danger of profanity is close at hand. Only in the realm of defilement may the act of sanctification be performed. The encounter between the spirit and the "other" is the origin of holiness. Holiness may evolve only where the spirit is in contact with its opposite. When the "ideal" begins to penetrate the kingdom of the "material," there is the beginning of sanctification. Where natural needs and urges become directed toward goals which may be acknowledged in the presence of God, and where spiritual aspirations become effective through their "communion" with the material sources of vitality, there alone may holiness be found. Only life is capable of holiness. Any ascetic rejection of the world of the senses excludes the possibility of sanctification. It is not the will that is holy, but the deed, because in it the spiritual and the material unite.[26] And it is through the holy deed alone that body as well as soul may be sanctified.

Our discussion of the meaning of the law within Judaism ought to be summed up at the close of this chapter. We may say now that the division of the laws of Judaism into rational or ethical laws and religious or ritual observances is not quite justified and, taken at face value, may be misleading. We have seen that even the so-called rational laws, concerning human conduct toward one's fellow, cannot derive their obligatory quality from reason. It is always a desire and a will that make a law obligatory; and the meaning of the revealed law in Judaism is that the law's obligatory nature derives from the expressed will of God.[27] This, of course, means that all the "rational" laws are also "religious" at the same time. Their justification may be reasonable; their reasonableness, however, is law for the Jew because of the divine command. Thus all the laws traditionally described as "between man and his fellow" (*bein adam l'havero*) have their place also in the category often referred to as "between man and God" (*bein adam lamakom*). One's conduct toward his neighbor is at the same time conduct toward God, and every hurt caused to another is also a sin against God.[28]

On the other hand, what appears to be purely religious observance has its ethical relevance through its indirect education of the material element in man. Through its creation of a physical awareness of an "other" and its demands, the system of religious observances educates the body for behavior that is not exclusively egocentric. The "purely religious," therefore, always has indirect influence on moral practice. In obeying the "ritual laws," which regulate the relationship between man and God, one indirectly brings greater order into one's relationships with other people. In a sense, by establishing habitual awareness of an "other," the indirect method achieves a measure of man's liberation. The claims on man which attempt to enslave him are innumerable—claims of his own nature, of economic forces, of social convention. But a system of law that teaches man to say a limited "no" to the promptings of his own nature and to the urgings of economic need, as well as to the dictatorship of social custom, and that at the same time develops within him an inclination to say "yes" to the commands of an authority that is not of this world, helps man to establish his independence in facing the world. Man is not required to refuse the claims of the world on him, but he may now withdraw himself from their pressure, and put some distance between himself and their importunings; he may now pause before committing himself. The discipline of living, which is one of the aims of religious observance, makes man free by enabling him to act in the world rather than react to it.[29]

However, the most important function of the "ritual laws" is the orientation to the divine which they achieve for the physical being of man. The commands of action (*mitzvot ma'asiyot*)[30] make it possible for the material element to enter into the relationship. From awareness of an "other," which is ethics, we proceed to the awareness of the "Wholly Other," which is religion.

It is on the level of religion that one may hope to overcome the dualism of human nature. Within ethics, the sensuous, impulsive nature of man has to surrender to the ethical command, which is foreign to it. On the religious level too, at first, the awareness of "the other," who is God, requires submission to the will of God, which is no less foreign to man's material nature than is the ethical command. However, on the religious level, the surrender to the will of God is the first phase of reconciliation and harmonization. As we saw, the religious insistence on relating the physical to God in submission to his command implied the vindication of physicality in its own right. The physical is, thus, accepted as meaningful and capable of guidance: It may seek its own fulfillment and yet serve the purpose that God has given man in the world. Only here, where the spirit need not deny the body and the body need not feel shame in the presence of the spirit, in the deed of unification between the two, may we find the culmination of all religious aspiration—the sanctification of life.

One may also put it this way. In the realm of ethics, the body of man is the servant or tool of the spirit. In the religious sphere, a measure of self-denial and submission is still demanded of the body; however, not as a mere tool of the spirit but for its own sake, so that—together with the spirit—the body too may participate in the religious experience of relatedness to God. This is the opening move in the overcoming of dualism. Both body and soul live in the presence of God. On the level of holiness, however, where the material in an act of self-realization can also do the will of God, one is almost inclined to say that the spirit becomes the servant of the body. Now, the spirit submits its own insights to be made use of in setting the direction for material self-affirmation.

It is important to appreciate that these various realms for which the law is significant do not exist independently of each other, nor can they be traversed by man one after the other. They represent the whole of man's responsibility. Man lives in all of them at the same time. They continually influence and sustain each other. The ethical, finding the source of its obligation in the will of God, depends on the religious. And since the human organism is the instrument of ethical action, its religious conditioning for submission to the will of God is itself important for the effectiveness of ethical conduct. On the other hand, the religious awareness of the "Wholly Other" is reached via the ethical awareness of an "other." Therefore, the more successful the ethical training by way of the "indirect method," the more promising the prospects of a physical awareness of the divine become. Every defeat in one realm is a defeat in all realms, and every achievement in one realm has its effect in all realms.

I do not mean to suggest that these various functions of the law are ever fully realized in the life of man; but they do reflect the direction which the Jewish way of life pursues, the goal at which it aims. According to rabbinical teaching, the Tora has been given in order to purify mankind.[31] When the task of purification is completed, the law will be fulfilled. In that state, to exercise "mercy, justice, and righteousness on earth" will have become the natural desire of the whole man. When, as the result of the sanctifying deed, mankind as a whole will "delight in these things," the law will no longer be needed. But there are no shortcuts in history. Only through the law will the law be overcome. When that phase is reached, mankind will have fulfilled its destiny, and history will be at an end.

III

DEED AND HISTORY

CHAPTER THIRTEEN

Israel

So far, we have discussed man as an individual. We have analyzed the different facets of his relationship with God and the world. We know, however, that the concept of Israel is essential for Judaism. Israel is not imaginable without Judaism; nor is Judaism, as a faith and way of life in the world, possible without Israel. All historical evidence proves that Israel is not a church but a people, a biological and political entity.[1]

This fact, however, raises several important questions: What need is there for the inclusion of a national idea in the ideological framework of Judaism? In what way does the religious experience require divine revelation to be granted to a people, and not only to individuals?[2] How does the service of God lead to a "chosen people" rather than to chosen personalities, elevated through their service? It is to these and related questions that we now turn.

From our preceding discussion, it follows that Judaism is not an "idealistic" or a "spiritual" religion, but a human one. It is a religion for the whole of man. It aims at relating life in its entirety to God. It is not, therefore, so much a religion of creed as it is the religion of the deed on earth.[3] The intellect or the soul may be satisfied with the creed; the whole man, however, may serve God only through the deed. The deed, as we saw, is born of the union of body and mind; in the deed alone may the two join together, complementing each other to mutual advantage.

The deed, however, is essentially social; and in order to be, it must find its place in the external world of man. It is social because it is always expressive of a relationship. Most intimately, it is the relationship between body and soul. The contribution of the body to the deed necessarily places the deed in the world outside of man. The deed, directed to the outside, is always in relationship to an "other." This other may be the world, a neighbor, or God. However, in order to be, the deed must be effective; and it must be so in the place where it belongs—in the external world, in history. In fact, the deed is the stuff of which history is made. As the deed of the race, so its history.

For the deed to be effective, it must not remain the act of an individual, but must become that of a community. The deed makes history if it is the materialization of the desire and will of a community of people joined together in a common cause. It is obvious that the community of the deed is not a church. A church is the outgrowth of that very dualism that Judaism aims to overcome: A church is essentially a community of believers and worshippers, a spiritual community; it is not foremost a community of doers. Because the deed is to be effective in the external world of man, the community that it requires must be a living society in reasonable control of its general order of life. This general order must be such that it will not render the deed of Judaism impossible or "unnatural."[4] Even the purely religious aspects of the Jewish deed are most intimately interwoven with community existence. If, for instance, the Sabbath were a purely spiritual day, to be observed in the heart alone through meditation and inner quiet, the economic structure of the society in which the Jew lived would have little or no bearing on its observance. But since the Sabbath, like any other *mitzva*, is a deed, requiring rest for the body as well as the soul, the economic order is of the utmost relevance, even for the purely religious significance of the day. The most conducive environment for the Sabbath is, therefore, a society whose economic and industrial activities are at a standstill on that day. The Sabbath is most naturally at home in such a society. Thus the Sabbath deed, to be most effective, of necessity strives for the coordination of its own intentions with the material fabric and order of the community. This, however, may be most powerfully accomplished by a community that possesses sufficient sovereignty to fashion the practical structure of its own life in accordance with its desires.

Innumerable examples could be found to illustrate the point from among the "ritual laws" alone. Of far greater interest in this connection, however, are the laws governing interpersonal relationships. These cover all the areas of man's life: Family and society, law and trade, education and industry, peace and war. Nothing affecting human intercourse is excluded from the scope of these commandments. As always in Judaism, the goal is not the entertainment of noble ideals, but their realization in the external world of action and conduct. Therefore, the full implementation of Judaism requires a society that is prepared to submit its whole life to the ordering will of Judaism. But a society sufficiently free to do so is not a congregation or a church, not a philosophical school or an exclusive club, not even a communion of saints, but a nation—a people in control of, at least, the internal order of its existence. The *mitzva* is a public deed, not a private one. One cannot be a Jew only "at heart"; one must be a Jew together with other Jews in history-making action.

A people in control of its own life, capable of implementing Judaism by applying it to the whole of life, is a people in its own land. Judaism, as the religion of the deed, requires a people in its land. The people alone can realize Judaism; in the land of the people alone may it be fully realized. Abraham was not the founder of a church, but the father of a people. "And I will make of you a great nation," God promises him at the beginning of his career, and he immediately directs Abraham "unto the land that I will show you."[5]

What has thus far been put pragmatically may also be expressed ideologically. The deed of the *mitzva* aims at oneness in life, at a measure of interpenetration between the spiritual and the material, and the transformation of both of these by lending material effectiveness to the spirit and spiritual directedness to the material and biologically vital. This dichotomy of the spiritual and the material is found everywhere in the world of man. The life of the community, as well as that of the individual, is infected through and through with the conflict between what "matters" but is without higher value, and what is of value but has no power to assert itself on its own. Wherever the dualism is encountered it should be overcome. What has been said of the individual also applies to society: Life in its entirety is to be placed in relationship to God. The attempt at "interpenetration" and "transformation" must be pursued on the group as well as the individual level. All the material aspects of society, its complete biophysical structure, are themselves in need of being invested with value and God-centeredness. But any group of people which is prepared to dedicate its corporate life to such a goal will emerge in history not only as a distinctive spiritual entity, but also as a political and biological unit—that is, as a distinctive national group. However, since its specific characteristics will be due to its determination to relate all the areas of its group life to God, it will properly be called a "people of God."

The historic mission of Israel has therefore been described by the Bible in the declaration: "And you shall be unto me a kingdom of priests, and a holy nation."[6] This kingdom of priests is not a society in which a priestly caste rules over an unpriestly populace in the name of some god. A holy nation is a realm in which all are priests. But where all are priests, all are servants—and God alone rules. A "kingdom of priests and a holy nation" is thus not a theocracy, but a God-centered republic.

It may now be shown how the concept of Israel as a holy nation not only does not conflict with the universalism of Israel's prophets, but actually leads to it as its own logical completion.[7]

The idea of a holy nation is not to be confused with that of nationalism. The goal of nationalism is to serve the nation; a holy nation serves God. The law of nationalism is national self-interest; the law of a kingdom of priests is the will of God. From the point of view of a nationalistic ideology, the nation is an end in itself; the holy nation is a means to an end. Since, however, the end is the wholeness of life in relationship to God, it obviously points beyond the national frame: The holy nation is the instrument for the realization of a supra-national purpose in history. The nation works toward a universal goal. As such, it does not exclude other nations; on the contrary, the end which it serves seeks the completion of its aspirations by means of these nations. The individual Jew does not live alone. Hence, if his deed is to be effective, he must unite with others in the common pursuit of Judaism's goal. The result is, inevitably, the "holy nation." But a holy nation cannot live in complete isolation. The more far-reaching the understanding that a people of God achieves with the rest of mankind, the more effective its deeds. The greater the understanding, the wider the area of life that becomes God-oriented. The deed is therefore always public: The deed of the individual takes place in his immediate society, in the midst of his people; and the deed of the nation is undertaken in the context of the life of the nations. As the individual must make common cause with the community, so the nation with the community of nations.

Realization through the holy people of necessity points to fuller realization through mankind.

The goal of Judaism is accomplished when it is reached by all mankind. Since, however, the goal is not essentially the teaching of noble ideals—which would indeed be rather easy, and ineffective—but rather their realization in history, one has to start with the smallest unit of living reality within which the deed of Judaism may become history-making; and such a unit is the nation. Individuals may teach; a people is needed in order to do effectively. Nationality here is not an ideological requirement, but a historical necessity. The gradual realization of the universal purpose in history is unable to dispense with the instrumentality of the holy nation. The universal purpose and its practical implementation in history determine the national characteristics of Israel. The "holy nation" is in fact the only people on earth whose very *raison d'etre* is the pursuit of a universal goal. It is the universalistic idea at the heart of Israel's existence which determines its national distinctiveness and uniqueness.

In history, he who seeks universalism cannot bypass the concept of the holy nation. Universalism is only an ideal, perhaps a potentiality; in reality, it has—thus far—never been known to exist. In reality, we have individuals and societies, nations and classes, empires and other concentrations of power and interest, all existing largely at cross-purposes with each other. A universal mankind will come into being only through the reconciliation of all separative interests, ambitions, and aspirations in the world. Reconciliation, however, means awareness of and care for the "other." This brings us back to our starting point: The obligation to care we found in the imitation of God; the effectiveness of the caring deed we saw safeguarded through the law of God. The harmony of mankind is the end-result in history of a development which starts with the individual *mitzva*, the deed of interpenetration of the spiritual and the material.

The God-orientation of the whole of the human being is the beginning of a process that aspires to a kind of universalism, or to what we have called the God-orientation of all life.

What is "last in deed" may of course be "first in thought"; in history, however, one cannot begin with mankind: One must start with man. One first builds humanity within oneself through an awareness of the other, which—implying a measure of reconciliation between body and soul within the individual—leads to the caring deed. But we render the individual deed effective by building humanity within the nation, by relating the entire scope of a relatively self-contained society to God. And one builds humanity by striving through the people for the final goal: To establish the world of mankind as the kingdom of God.[8]

The holy nation is properly called the chosen people. The idea expresses, first of all, the practical necessity of a national instrument for the realization of the supra-national goal. This world will be established as a kingdom of God when *all* the nations submit to the will of God. But before all nations will do so, one must do so. The "kingdom of priests" is the necessary pathfinder and forerunner of the kingdom of God. If the universal goal is to be accomplished in history, there must be a stage known as "his first fruits of the increase."[9]

The rise of God's "first fruits," however, cannot be left altogether to natural growth. We have seen that the obligation of any law derives not from its rationality, but from the expressed will of a law-giving authority. Therefore, the will of God exists and is obligatory for man only insofar as it has been made known to him.[10] The will of God revealed to individuals is law for them as individuals. While it is correct, as we have maintained, that in order to be effective in history, individuals must join in a common cause, it is nevertheless true that if the will of God were proclaimed to them as individuals only, their decision to act in unity of purpose would be logical, but not the fulfillment of a divine command. Unless the will of God is directed to the people as such, the dualism between individual obligation and national interest remains unresolved. Religion then becomes the domain of individual souls, whereas the nation as such remains free to be guided by the realism of its self-interest. To submit the entire structure of a people's life to the will of God is a national obligation only if the will of God has been revealed to the people as a whole. Only because God addressed himself to the people is the fulfillment of his will a national responsibility for Israel.

It is, however, not altogether irrelevant to consider that Israel was not really "chosen," but rather came into being by having been chosen. God never chose the Jews; rather, any people whom God chose was to become the Jewish people. The choice of God made Israel. Why was one family singled out, and not another? Why did God address himself to one specific tribe, and not to all the nations of the earth at once? Is it because only among this tribe did he first encounter the personalities who were best qualified to become the patriarchs of a proposed holy nation? In answer one may ask: Who would fathom the mind of the Almighty? Let it suffice for us to recognize that a "people of God" is a practical requirement for the penetration of the divine purpose into the history of man— for the fulfillment of man's destiny on earth as intended by the revealed will of the Creator. As to the rest, Jews can only testify to what has happened to them. They have been called into being by the will of God. They have been fashioned and formed through their national encounters with the divine Presence.

CHAPTER FOURTEEN

God in History

Just as the individual does not live alone, neither does a people. For this reason, as long as the holy people remains the "one people" in history, its deeds will be, at best, only partially effective. Its success or failure will depend on the international constellation in which the people lives and strives for its goal. A people with a purpose of its own, even though the purpose be an essentially universal one, may find itself at odds with other peoples, which are guided by exclusively self-serving considerations. Indeed, the *raison d'etre* of a God-centered nation would of necessity clash with the life-motifs of a world of self-centered nations. The conflict, at times, is unavoidable, and can have tragic consequences for the "one people." In the history of Israel, these consequences are responsible for the exile; they have created the wandering Jew.

In one sense, exile is a natural phenomenon. For millennia, the way of life of the "one people" has been at cross-purposes with that of the rest of the world. Israel could easily have come to terms with Assyria and Rome, with Mohammed and even Torquemada, if only it had been willing to surrender its own distinctive purpose in history. Because in moments of ultimate trial Israel was not prepared to betray its destiny as the people of God, waves of hatred and destruction have swept over it unceasingly. Exile is not an accident, but the natural lot of the people of God. Jewish history is inseparable from world history: The intensity of the exile is the measure of the world's opposition to the aspirations of the God-centered people. It is the negative version of Jewish universalism. Israel is always as homeless in this world as God's purpose for man is in exile in history. The exile of Israel is one of the manifestations of *galut hashechina*, the exile of the divine Presence from the affairs of men. It is true that in a mood of rigorous self-criticism, Israel uttered the words: "Because of our sins we have been exiled from our land." This is indeed a valid statement when the Jewish people faces God. Facing the world, however, the truth has been formulated in the phrase, "for your sake are we killed all the day."[1] From the very outset of its history, Israel knew that exile would be inseparable from loyalty to its God-oriented course.[2]

The nature of Israel's exile, the intensity of Jewish homelessness, has always been the measuring rod for the moral and spiritual maturity of the world around the Jew. The wanderings of the Jewish people, through lands and times, are the most revealing records of the ethical and religious history of the non-Jewish world. As was the case with their first exile in Egypt, so, too, were most of the subsequent exiles of the children of Israel not God-ordained punishments but humanly imposed persecutions. The question has thus been raised by Jews and Gentiles alike: If the immeasurable burden of suffering that is the exile is indeed undeserved, why does God allow it to happen? Why does he not protect the innocent? Why does he not intervene in time and strike down the would-be persecutor before he is able to perpetrate his crimes?

Such questions assume that a certain form of intervention in the course of history would be proper for the Almighty. Now, if such divine intervention on behalf of the innocent were the observable rule in history, then the suffering of Israel through the ages would prove something. But the suffering of the materially weak and guiltless seems to be rather the norm in history. So we may say that the exile conforms to the norm, and that the problem of exile is, therefore, but a specific aspect of the general problem of theodicy. However prominent and incomparable an example of undeserved suffering the exile of the Jews may be, it is not the only case of its kind. He who asks why God permits the people of God to be persecuted might as well ask why God allows any injustice to be inflicted on any of his creatures. Why does God tolerate any suffering of the innocent in his creation? Such questions are, of course, as old as recorded history.[3]

The problem of theodicy, of God's justice, exists in two forms. For the purposes of our discussion we shall call them the cosmic and the historical-ethical aspects. There is evil, or imperfection, which seems to be congenital to creation itself. This is the cosmic aspect of the problem of theodicy, which was discussed earlier in the context of creation.[4] Now, however, we are concerned with evil as it is introduced into history by conscious, created beings—as the work of men and nations. And the question is, why does God not prevent man from spreading misery and sorrow in creation?

In answer to the problem, it has rightly been pointed out that any specific intervention on the part of God would not only render the doing of evil impossible, but would eliminate the foundations of all ethical action as well.[5] In a world in which evil would be doomed to complete and manifest failure from the outset, goodness could not prosper either. One cannot frighten people into goodness. In order to be good, man must choose the good; but there is choice only where there is freedom. In order to be good, then, man must be free to be wicked; he must be permitted to choose between good and evil. Where there is no practical possibility of choosing evil successfully, there is no opportunity to espouse the good. The goodness of man consists in his free commitment to the good. When we discussed the cosmic aspect of the problem, we found that an imperfect creation was freedom's only opportunity. But what is true of creation in this context is also valid for God's continued relation to the history of the human race. No doubt, God is sufficiently powerful to intervene every time a wrong is committed; it would indeed be a small matter for him to eliminate all evil and injustice from the earth. But his *evident* intervention would destroy not only evil, but also the essence of man's humanity—namely, his moral responsibility. Man is man only if he may choose between alternative courses of action, and if he can do so in moral freedom.

One may also put it this way: Why ask for continuous miracles to rectify what goes wrong in the world? Would it not be simpler to ask for the creation of a perfect man, who would be so endowed by nature as to be incapable of committing any evil? The answer, of course, is even simpler than the question is naive. A perfect man is, in this sense, a contradiction in terms; it is an impossibility. A man incapable of doing wrong would not be human. The imperfection of human nature is inseparable from its most significant asset: Its potential for goodness, its capacity for responsible decision and action. Having created man as a morally responsible being, God had to grant him the opportunity for ethical action. The action itself must remain man's own choice, or else its ethical quality is lost.[6] Man must be able to go wrong if he is to go right at all—such is the perpetual risk inherent in the human situation. The possibility of humanly inflicted suffering, undeservedly imposed on other human beings, is always present in history, as long as man, in God's unfathomable wisdom, is permitted to seek his own fulfillment.

We may now approach once again the problem of the measureless injustice that is implied in the long centuries of Israel's exile. Exile, as we saw, is the outcome of an unavoidable conflict between the historic function of the "one people" and the ambitions of the other nations. As such, exile is a symptom that constructive, universal reconciliation is still lacking in the world. The subhuman excesses of hatred and cruelty to which Israel has been exposed, almost without respite, are themselves the measure of the impotence of the spirit and the blind fury of the self-centered passions of man's biophysical inheritance. They bear convincing witness to the tragic truth that "humanity" is still only a potentiality, and far from being a reality; that the deed of transformation, rendering the spiritual vital and the vital spiritually purposeful, the *mitzva*, has still not become effective in history. And yet, God does not manifestly intervene. History is man's responsibility. The task is man's, for only man can build mankind. Only man can overcome the dualism within himself; only if he does so himself is it overcome. Of course, God is omnipresent. If he wished to, he could miraculously destroy the tyrant or the guilty nation. But would such an act of God create reconciliation among human beings? Would it establish mankind? Certainly it would create fear, and no nation would dare lift up the sword against another—and thus all history would end in universal trembling. In every miracle, history is at a standstill. But the stuff of history is the deed of man. Responsibility and purpose in history have been entrusted into his hands.

I do not mean to suggest that what has been said here with regard to God's silence in history is the solution to the problem of theodicy. It is, however, an important step forward to understand that the problem is not merely the result of human ignorance, but is implanted in the scheme of things. If divine providence were indeed manifest in the world, if it convincingly lived up to human expectations, as it were, and if God acted always as man's sense of justice would have him do, the overwhelming evidence that "sin doesn't pay" would extinguish man's freedom to commit himself to one or another possible course of action. There would be only "goodness" left, imposed from without. Man would cease to be a morally

responsible creature. Therefore the problem of God's providence and justice must forever remain unsolved in history, so as
to enable the possibility of history itself, and of life's increasing
orientation to God, through human responsibility.

Once again we may point to the concept of the hiding God,
which was discussed in the first part of this work.[7] We saw that
the original religious experience of the encounter had to be
momentary in order to be endured by man; and even while it
lasted, the divine Presence could reveal itself only from behind
some protective barrier, or else man could not have survived
the terror of the Almighty. We also saw that the encounters had
to be extremely rare in history in order to leave room for doubt
and, thus, to safeguard man's spiritual freedom, which is the
most noble quality of faith. God hides from man most of the
time so that man may believe in him without compulsion. We
further noted the religious need for the impossibility of proving
God's existence intellectually. Any such inescapable proof would
put the human intellect in chains, prejudicing its search for
truth. Finally, we have found yet another meaning of the concept of theodicy: For the sake of man, God cannot *evidently*
interfere in the course of history, for such intervention would
completely crush man's moral independence and responsibility.
As the prophet said of him: "He will be silent in his love."[8] The
very silence of God in history is due to his concern for man.

Does this mean, then, that God has left his creation completely
to its own devices, allowing things to take their course as they
may? Such a thought would be incompatible with the responsibility of which the Creator cannot, in any imaginable way,
divest himself. Things need not happen in accordance with
human insight and expectation, yet there is an ultimate responsibility that is God's. By creating man as a being in need of
spiritual, intellectual, and ethical freedom in order to fulfill

himself, God took a chance. In respecting man's God-given—
though limited—independence, the Creator incurs a risk. Man
is responsible to the extent to which he is free; God is responsible to the extent to which he has made man free and sustains
man in freedom. For this reason alone it is inconceivable that
God departed from his creation and is indifferent to what man
does with his life and the world.

The encounter, as well as the revealed law of God, is of
course in itself a direct indication of the Creator's interest. At
the same time, the need for divine silence in history excludes
only manifest intervention; it does not eliminate indirect intervention by the Almighty. Such indirect, and therefore not altogether convincing, intervention in the affairs of men, which the
human being is free to recognize or to reject, may well be one
of the ways in which God discharges his responsibility to his
creation. It may be a counterbalance to the risk of freedom that
is inherent in life and in history. For all we know, God may
even intervene in the guise of natural events, which happen in
accordance with natural laws. Many of these events are his
invisible or unrecognized messengers.[9]

It is not inconceivable, however, that as a result of human
action, performed in freedom, or of the interplay of natural
forces—and at times a combination of the two—a situation may
arise in which divine intervention may have to be direct and
manifest to all. When, for instance, the intended outcome of
history is in utter jeopardy—not to mention other imaginable
possibilities—the evident act of God may be quite in keeping
with what is dictated by God's own responsibility. In such cases
we speak of miracles. The miracle may be one of God's ways to
safeguard the intended ultimate outcome. As the human deed is
a manifestation of human responsibility met in freedom, similarly—although on an incomparably higher level—the miracle
is an expression of divine freedom in the service of divine
responsibility. At times, when the deed fails, the miracle may be

the only corrective. This, of course, means that miracles are not the ideal way of influencing the destinies of men. Only the deed is according to plan; the miracle is a stopgap in history. Not only is history at a standstill in the miracle, but the miracle is a sign of a serious breakdown in history. The need for the miracle stems from the measure of freedom that is inherent in creation. When freedom, misused, threatens to overstep the limits of the calculated risk God took with his creation, the freedom of the Almighty may have to bring its trespassing to a halt. It is, of course, not for man to say when a situation has arisen that must be salvaged by a miracle. Let us suffice with the idea that there is, indeed, a place for the miracle within the natural scheme of things.

Another question, however, may also be expected at this stage: While the logical and ethical necessity for the miracle may be conceded, is not the materialization of a miracle a practical impossibility? If the question means to imply that miracles are impossible because they are contrary to the laws of nature, we must regard it as completely devoid of meaning. We need not enter here into a discussion of the numerous religious and philosophical rationalizations of the miracle which, rather than interpret the concept, simply explain it away. The deist David Hume was perfectly right when, in defining the miracle, he maintained that the determining factor was not that an event occurred contrary to the observable laws of nature, but that it happened as the result of a direct intervention by God.[10] Putting it this way implies that not all miracles need be observable as such. At the same time, Hume's definition does say that miracles are contrary to nature. After all, direct divine intervention is not natural. A miracle is in essence—although not always in appearance—unnatural. Nevertheless, it is a poor contribution to the discussion to maintain that on this account alone a miracle could not happen. What is contrary to nature is, of course, *naturally* impossible. No one who is prepared to give credence to the possibility of miracles ever denied that fact. Indeed, the point of the affirmation of the miracle is that the naturally impossible may happen as the result of divine intervention. The real issue, therefore, is not whether what is contrary to natural law is within the realm of natural possibility, but whether a form of direct intervention on the part of God is conceivable or not.

Obviously, the possibility of such intervention cannot be denied on the basis of God's lack of power. Starting with the premise of an almighty Creator, it does not seem logical to deny God the might to act within his creation. As long as we consider nature a thing apart from God, as we indeed do when we see it as creation, not even a strictly deterministic interpretation of its laws will rule out the possibility of the miracle. That nothing within nature may disrupt the chain of cause and effect does not prove that the God of nature may not do it. We ought to understand the philosophical significance of a position that rejects any form of direct divine intervention. There is, indeed, no way of establishing the *practical* impossibility of the miracle. The miracle may only be rejected for logical reasons as being incompatible with the premises of certain forms of metaphysics.

Such logical rejection follows, for instance, from the position of pantheism. Assuming, for example, the Stoic contention that the laws of nature are identical with the laws of reason, or with those of a universal pneuma that is the soul of the universe, no intervention by God in the flow of events is conceivable. Such intervention would indicate that the laws of universal reason were somewhere faulty and in need of correction. Quite within the Stoic tradition, Spinoza wrote: "For whatsoever is contrary to nature is also contrary to reason, and whatsoever is contrary to reason is absurd, and, *ipso facto*, to be rejected."[11] For Spinoza, of course, the cosmos becomes absorbed in God. The identification is so complete that nature disappears as a separate entity. There is only the infinite substance, which is deity. Starting with such concepts, Spinoza must conclude that "the power and efficiency of nature are in themselves the divine power and efficiency." The laws of nature are themselves the will of God; they are his decrees, "following from the necessity and perfection of the Divine nature."[12] Miracles, therefore, would be contrary not only to the laws of nature, but also to divine nature itself.

There is also, however, a form of theistic metaphysics from which the rejection of the miracle follows as a logical necessity. Assuming that creation was perfect, representing a divine order in completion, the need for a miracle would reveal a flaw in what was originally planned to be without blemish. The corrective measure of the miracle would indicate that a "slip-up" had occurred in the divine order. It would be no less absurd to entertain such a possibility on the basis of the premises outlined than it would be to accept Spinoza's assumption that anything contrary to reason could never occur in nature.

The Spinozistic argument against the miracle need not detain us longer. Spinoza's reasoning is cogent, but only as long as we grant his acosmic pantheism. As discussed earlier, the very essence of religion is the confrontation between man and God.[13] The religious experience of the encounter and the idea of creation are diametrically opposed to any form of pantheism. Thus, far from agreeing with Spinoza's dictum that "the power and efficiency of nature are in themselves the divine power and efficiency," we can conceive of creation only as an act of divine self-limitation. Nature, as creation, is apart from God; it is outside him, it is "the other" to him. The laws of nature may indeed be called the decrees of the Creator, but they are not, as pantheism understands them, identical with the divine will. The laws of nature are nature's laws; they are not divine but natural, which is to say created. There is no logical contradiction between such a concept of natural laws and the possibility of divine intervention in them.

What is more, we have found that creation as such must be conceived as being, of necessity, imperfect.[14] Now, in a perfect universe—if such a universe were possible—a miracle could never happen: All intervention with perfection can only be destructive. Nor would there be any need for the miracle in such a universe. It was in the very imperfection of the creation that we discovered both the challenge for man and the source of his freedom to meet that challenge. Within perfection there is no choice, no alternative, no freedom. The imperfection of creation is man's opportunity. This same opportunity granted to man in the form of freedom and responsibility may in history necessitate the corrective act of the miracle. As the element of imperfection is the chance for human freedom, how much more may it serve as the thin end of the wedge for divine intervention.[15]

While the miracle may be the divine corrective, man's destiny on earth can be fulfilled only by man himself. The task and the responsibility are his. A man made good by a miracle is not a good man, but a good puppet. The essence of goodness, as we saw, is expressed in an attitude or action consciously undertaken by man without outside compulsion. If the creation of "mankind" consists, as we have argued, in the achievement of universal reconciliation, it can be accomplished only by man himself. Unless reconciliation is an actual experience brought about by human desire—unless it means fellowship fostered by man through his own exertions—it cannot exist. And even the day of which the prophet says, "And the Eternal shall be King over all the earth; On that day shall the Eternal be One, and his name one,"[16] cannot be the Eternal's doing alone, without reference to man's success or failure in history. If it were altogether the work of the Eternal, it would have been more logical to dispense with all history from the very beginning and start with the day on which "the Eternal shall be King." There is a share of human responsibility in making the Eternal King over all the earth by placing all life under his sovereignty. The striving for this goal is the meaning of history.

Man's redemption is, therefore, within the scope of human responsibility. That is how God willed it. While "mankind," established through the self-redemption of man, is always far removed in the future, in history one may discern its emerging outlines in the interdependence of all human destinies. No one lives in "splendid isolation"; all have their neighbors, and whatever one does, or leaves undone, affects others and, in some measure, all. These facts point to the common responsibility of the race of men. Because of the interdependence of all life, the righteous, too, suffer from the consequences of the deeds of the wicked; this reflects the reality of mankind in its negative state. That we are tied to each other from the beginning is the sign that we should join each other in the end. Universal redemption is the common responsibility of all.

This should not, of course, be taken to suggest that man is entirely on his own. He who knows of the encounter and the revelation of the law is sure of God's concern and care, with which history, as man's creation of mankind, is initiated. He also knows that even in those long stretches of human history during which God seems to be silent, he is in fact "silent in his love."[17] In the boldness of faith, man may often recognize the hints of the workings of the hiding God—not to mention those rare moments when man is overwhelmed by more convincing signs of divine concern. The rabbis of the Talmud were right to view man as a "partner" of God in the works of creation.[18] Who would say where the work of God comes to an end and the human contribution begins? Man may be "as nothing" before God, yet God nonetheless desires man's partnership.

The goal of human history may never be achieved, the unity of mankind may never become a complete reality, and the day on which "the Eternal shall be King over all the earth" may yet require a culminating act of divine grace and love; but man's own responsibility never ceases, for his opportunity to bring the goal closer to realization is never lost. As long as man lives, his failure cannot be final. For after every failure, not only can he be forgiven, but he may even start anew, if he "returns." After every failure, *teshuva*, or return, allows man to continue as if the failure had been a success. The return to God is an act of complete transformation of character. In the act of *teshuva*, the past is not undone—which would be impossible—but redone. The impact of past failures becomes creative in its effect on future desire and action. The man who returns to God incorporates even his past sins into the structure of his reborn personality. Moreover, man is forever invited to return.[19] Universal reconciliation may never be achieved by man alone, yet it is always *achievable* by him. Because of *teshuva*, the hope for redemption is never forfeited.[20]

What, however, ensures that man will make use of the gift of *teshuva*; that, after his numerous and tragic failures, he will seek the way of return to God? What ensures that, in a fit of universal folly and criminality, he will not extinguish life itself from the face of the earth and thus commit his final blunder? In a sense, we have already answered this question. God, in endowing man with a measure of freedom—the source of all human folly, and all human achievement—accepted responsibility for the final outcome. God alone, who determined the beginning, will determine the end. Having granted man the freedom to fail, God will not let him fail irrevocably. The divine responsibility for creation is the guarantee that the purpose of man's formation in freedom and responsibility will not ultimately be thwarted. That is the root of the messianic faith. God's intention for man, as revealed in the encounter and by his law, will be fulfilled. It is the messianic promise, inseparable from history. But only the goal is preordained; the path to it, however, must be blazed by man, and the time required to reach it will depend on him. What the Sages said of Israel applies to the entire race: They will not be redeemed unless they return.[21] Since in the final reckoning God will not be defeated, there is always time to return. And so we have ample failure in ample time, which means ample suffering. The hope of man is that, through suffering, he will return to be redeemed. But redeemed he will be, for God lives.

The messianic fulfillment of history is beyond any doubt. The most convincing indication of this is the survival of Israel. The survival of Judaism and of the Jewish people in all times, in conditions of utter political and material weakness, in spite of continuous persecution, and in defiance of an endless series of the most barbarous attempts at their extermination, defies all explanation. It is the mystery of the ages. The return of Israel to its ancient homeland in our days, as Israel maintained for numberless generations that it would do, is incomparable in human history. As a manifestation of the interdependence of all life, Israel's suffering is the measure of man's failure to become a partner with God in the task of human salvation. Israel is always as close to martyrdom as the human race is removed from humanity. On the other hand, Israel's survival is itself the proof that God's purpose in history will not be defeated, and that the day of mankind's reconciliation will yet dawn.

Whether the price that must be paid in terms of suffering and misery will be well worth the achievement is not within man's ability either to affirm or to deny. Judging from the standpoint of experience, the rabbis of the Talmud have said: "It would have been better for man not to be created"; yet they nevertheless accepted life as a task and a responsibility, for they continued: "However, now that he has been created, let him look to his deeds."[22] Only one who knows of the original intention that moved God in creating may judge the road as well as the destination. We may have some hint of God's own purpose for man, as revealed to man by God; yet we can know nothing of God's purpose with his creation as a whole. Being placed in this world, man has been invited to accept, and to cooperate with, what God desires for him. Let this suffice.

Indeed, before the day of fulfillment and universal salvation arrives, many will have suffered because of the sins of others; many will have fallen by the wayside. What of them? What of the numberless millions who pay the price for the risk that God has taken with creation, but never live to see the day of justification? One can answer only by saying that our concept of divine justice demands that on the day of universal fulfillment, they, too, must be vindicated and justified individually, just as they suffered individually. Divine justice, which is one of the ways we have conceived of God's care for man, is the postulate of immortality. It requires that in the act of final redemption, all generations that were ever born be redeemed.[23] Even the dead must live to share in the realization of the promise that alone justifies the travail of all times.

God, as he has made himself known to man, is a caring God. God is our surety that nothing that has value, in accordance with his desire for man, ever perishes. He is the Preserver. Because he is, we know that no good deed and no kind word, no noble thought and no sincere striving for the good, are ever in vain. Because he is God, nothing worth preserving is ever so lost in history as not to be found again—be it even beyond history.[24]

Notes

CHAPTER ONE

1. Saadia Gaon, writing on the purpose of his work in the opening chapter of *The Book of Doctrines and Beliefs*, says: "I saw men sink, as it were, in a sea of doubt and covered by the waters of confusion..." Saadia Gaon, *The Book of Doctrines and Beliefs*, trans. Alexander Altmann (Oxford: East and West Library, 1946), p. 29.

Similarly, Maimonides, elaborating on his reason for composing *The Guide of the Perplexed*, writes: "He [the educated religious man] will thus fall into confusion and be faced by a dilemma: Either he follows his reason and rejects those expressions [of anthropomorphic description of the Godhead] as he understands them: Then he will think that he is rejecting the dogmas of our religion. Or else he continues to accept them in the way he has been taught and refuses to be guided by his reason. He thus brusquely turns his back on his own reason, and yet he cannot help feeling that his faith has been gravely impaired." Moses Maimonides, *The Guide of the Perplexed*, trans. Chaim Rabin, introduction and commentaries by Julius Guttmann (London: East and West Library, 1952), Maimonides' introduction, p. 41.

2. This, of course, does not apply fully to Saadia. It is very likely that he is much closer to our time than we usually assume. His method is far more scientific than rationalistic.

3. Maimonides, *Guide of the Perplexed* 3:54.

4. Maimonides, *Guide of the Perplexed*, Maimonides' introduction and 1:34.

5. Maimonides, *Guide of the Perplexed* 3:51.

6. Maimonides, *Guide of the Perplexed* 3:52.

7. Cf. Wilhelm Windelband, *A History of Philosophy* (New York: Macmillan, 1923), p. 282.

8. Cf. Saadia Gaon, *Book of Doctrines and Beliefs*, pp. 95, 103, 123; Maimonides, *Guide of the Perplexed* 1:34 (p. 61) and see also the note by Guttmann, p. 208.

Cf. also Thomas Aquinas, *Summa Contra Gentiles*, trans. Anton C. Pegis (Garden City, N.Y.: Image Books, 1955), 1:4, pp. 66–68.

9. G.E. Lessing, *The Education of the Human Race*, trans. Fred W. Robertson (London: Kegan Paul, 1896).

10. Immanuel Kant, *Religion Within the Limits of Reason Alone* (New York: Harper, 1960), p. 142.

11. Quoted after Max Scheler, *On the Eternal in Man*, trans. Bernard Noble (New York: Harper, 1960).

12. See Julius Guttmann, *Philosophies of Judaism*, trans. David A. Silverman (Philadelphia: Jewish Publication Society, 1964), p. 325.

13. Hermann Cohen, *The Religion of Reason Out of the Sources of Judaism*, trans. Simon Kaplan (New York: Ungar, 1972).

14. *Vernunftsverhältnis.*

15. See Cohen, *Religion of Reason*, ch. iv, pp. 71–84. It may be of interest to recall here Moses Mendelssohn's attempt to solve the problem. When he maintained that the purpose of the revelation at Sinai was not to provide any intellectual insight, but rather to establish a law as the command of God, he very nearly stumbled on the possibility of establishing the independence of religion. He failed, however, because the separate realm that he claimed for religion was founded not so much on his interpretation of religion as on his evaluation of reason. The universality of reason, Mendelssohn assumed, excluded the possibility that any rational insight could have been reserved for one particular people at a specific time. He did not require of religion what religion is by its own nature, but rather allowed his concept of reason to dictate what religion ought to be.

16. Cf. Scheler, *Eternal in Man*, p. 132.

17. Maimonides, *Guide of the Perplexed* 1:58.

18. See Guttmann, *Philosophies of Judaism*, p. 231; Hasdai Crescas, *Light of the Eternal* (Jerusalem: Ramot, 1990), 1:3, 3, pp. 99–115. [Hebrew]

19. F.H. Bradley has this to say on the subject: "A mere negation is unmeaning. To deny, except from a basis of positive assumption, is quite impossible... And, in the second place, we must remember that what is denied is, nonetheless, somehow predicated on our Absolute..." F.H. Bradley, *Appearance and Reality: Metaphysical Essay* (New York: Macmillan, 1925), p. 243.

20. Philo, *On the Posterity of Cain*, in *Philosophical Writings: Philo*, ed. Hans Lewy (Oxford: East and West Library, 1946), p. 64.

21. Philo, *On Flight and Finding*, in *Philosophical Writings*, p. 66; cf. also p. 64.

22. Philo, *Posterity of Cain*, p. 64.

23. In vain does Hermann Cohen, in the third chapter of *Religion of Reason*, attempt to show, with the help of Kant's doctrine of categories, that Maimonides meant to establish by the negative attributes God's function as the Creator, a function related intrinsically to his essence and following directly from it. Maimonides was not a Kantian *a la* Cohen; according to Maimonides, the idea of creation does not follow logically from the divine essence, nor is there— precisely because of that essence—any possibility of a relationship between God and the world. See Maimonides, *Guide of the Perplexed* 1:52 and 2:25.

24. Immanuel Kant, *Critique of Judgment*, trans. Werner S. Pluhar (Indianapolis: Hackett, 1987), "General Comment on Teleology," pp. 369–381.

25. See Windelband, *History of Philosophy*, p. 225.

26. Cf. Gershom Scholem, *Major Trends in Jewish Mysticism* (New York: Schocken, 1941), p. 24.

27. Like John Locke centuries after him, Judah Halevi lets reason function as a negative criterion of revelation. Accordingly, he maintains that while there is no need for agreement between reason and

revelation, neither can there be anything in the Tora that is contrary to reason. See Judah Halevi, *Kuzari* 1:67 and also 1:9.

CHAPTER TWO

1. See Immanuel Kant, *Critique of Pure Reason*, trans. Norman Kemp Smith (New York: St. Martin's, 1965), p. 433 (A685/B713).

2. On the significance of such "proofs" for religious faith, cf. pp. 44-48.

3. Aristotle, *Metaphysics* 12:9; Aristotle, *On the Soul* 3:6.

4. Aristotle, *Metaphysics* 13:7.

5. One of the major inconsistencies in Maimonides' thought stems from his solution to the problem of providence. At first he maintains, as follows logically from his adoption of the Neo-Platonic concept of the undefinable One, that there is no possibility of any relationship between God and anything created. See Maimonides, *Guide of the Perplexed* 1:52. This would then eliminate providence; providence is, of course, relationship. But such a conclusion was unacceptable for Maimonides, the believing Jew. And so he took from the Muslim Aristotelians the illegitimate combination of Aristotelian Active Intellect and Neo-Platonism. The Active Intellect, by means of Neo-Platonic emanation, allows for a bond between man as a rational being and God. See Maimonides, *Guide of the Perplexed* 3:17-18.

6. "If such Gods as there may be have no care for us, and pay no regard to our actions, what becomes of piety and religion?" Cicero, *Nature of the Gods* 1:2.

7. Cf. Cohen, *Religion of Reason*, pp. 71-84.

8. Deuteronomy 4:35.

9. A case in point is Genesis 28:21. It would not be difficult to show that, throughout the entire Bible, the phrases "the Eternal is my God," "I shall be a God unto you," and others like them normally refer to divine care and providence.

10. The meaning of the encounter seems to be the key to understanding the book of Job. For many long chapters the problem of

theodicy is analyzed critically. Job cannot accept any of the solutions offered by his friends. Finally, in the climax toward which the entire discussion has been leading, "The Eternal replied to Job out of the tempest and said…" (Job 38:1) With bated breath we await the answer—only to be disappointed; apparently, no answer is forthcoming. God elaborates on his unlimited might and wisdom and the ignorance and insignificance of Job. All this, however, seems to be pointless; it was never doubted by Job. He was confused only because he was unable to discern justice in the divine government. What answer is given to the doubts of man? And still, Job seems to have recognized the answer. He who was originally fearless in his criticism is now at peace.

11. Cf., for example, Rashi's interpretation of Hillel's famous saying: That which is hateful to you, do not do to your friend. "Your friend," explains Rashi, "is God." See Shabbat 31a.

12. Here we differentiate between the fact of revelation, which is the encounter proper, and its contents, which are the word of God. In this part of the discussion, our concern is mainly with the fact of revelation and its analysis. The interpretation of the content of revelation will be offered in the second section of this work.

Chapter Three

1. As we observed, the idea of the encounter is not logically compatible with either the Aristotelian First Cause or the Neo-Platonic One, or, for that matter, with any other variation of the metaphysical Absolute. But, as was noted, neither of these terms is the biblical premise. We know of the God of the Bible only insofar as we know of the encounter.

2. Even then it is a mere statement of faith, based on the assumption—which cannot be proven experimentally—that nature is both rational and uniform. Cf., for example, J.W.N. Sullivan, *The Bases of Modern Science* (Penguin Pelican, 1939), p. 11; also A.N. Whitehead, *Science and the Modern World* (New York: New American Library, 1956), especially the first three chapters.

3. By now, this ought to be generally accepted, especially as a result of the works of both David Hume and Immanuel Kant.

4. Cf. Kant, *Critique of Pure Reason*, p. 525 (A631/B659).

5. Positivism, if it claims to be more than what it really is, i.e., a working hypothesis for the laboratory, is exactly what it denies to be possible, namely a brand of metaphysics, and a very poor one at that.

6. Morris R. Cohen, *A Preface to Logic* (London: Routledge, 1946), p. 58.

7. The quotation marks seem to be required by the complete dissolution of all solid objects into events in modern scientific theory.

8. Cf., for example, Heisenberg's Principle of Indeterminacy in nuclear physics, which really means that, when dealing with the speed and the entities of atomic structure, all observation is a form of interference. The scientist cannot eliminate himself completely from the context of the events observed, and, therefore, the ideal of scientific exactitude is not realizable.

9. On the need for divine protection and preservation of human individuality against divine omnipotence, cf. chapter four.

10. Cf. pp. 48-50.

11. Jeremiah 20:7-9.

12. Cf. Saadia Gaon, *Book of Doctrines and Beliefs*, p. 112.

13. Isaiah 43:10. The midrash interpreted the words boldly by saying: "When you are my witnesses, I am God; but when you are not my witnesses, I am—as it were—not God." See Sifrei Deuteronomy 33:5.

CHAPTER FOUR

1. Cf. chapter two.

2. Exodus 3:6.

3. Deuteronomy 4:33.

4. Cf. *The Song of God: Bhagavad-Gita* (New York: Mentor Books, 1954), ch. xi, p. 92.

5. Deuteronomy 4:24.

6. See chapter two.

7. Ezekiel 3:23-24.

8. Cf. Megila 19b, where R. Hiya bar Aba says in the name of R. Yohanan: "Had there been in the cave in which Moses and Elijah stood even as small an opening as the point of a needle, it would not have been possible [for either of them] to stand there on account of the brilliance of the light; for it is written... 'man shall not see me and live' (Exodus 33:20)."

9. Isaiah 45:15. We ought to distinguish between God's "hiding himself" and the notion of God "hiding his face." In the encounter, God does "face" man; it is the divine essence which is veiled or hidden, so that man may "face" God. The "hiding of the face," on the other hand, is the opposite of the encounter. The "hiding God" is essential for the relationship; the "hiding of the face" indicates a breakdown in the relationship and the withdrawal of the divine concern.

10. Cf. Rudolf Otto, *The Idea of the Holy: An Inquiry into the Non-Rational Factor in the Idea of the Divine and Its Relation to the Rational*, trans. John W. Harvey (New York: Oxford, 1958), ch. iv, pp. 12-24.

11. Psalms 138:6.

12. Isaiah 66:1-2; quotation based on the 1917 edition of the Jewish Publication Society.

13. Megila 31a.

14. Genesis 18:25, 27. Rudolf Otto, in his work *The Idea of the Holy*, speaks of man's realization that he is but "dust and ashes" as the Abrahamic experience (cf. pp. 9, 21). What Otto does not seem to recognize is the truly surprising aspect of the experience: That "dust and ashes" has the moral independence to face God and to plead with him. Nor does Otto see with sufficient clarity the Jewish concept that whatever intimation man may have of God as the "Wholly Other" must somehow be communicated to him. But where there is communication, the "Wholly Other" is made accessible to man. For the same reason, a Jew will not be able to accept Otto's idea that the *kreaturgefuhl* (the "dust-and-ashes" experience) leads to the predication of all reality to the Godhead and its denial for the creature. This might indeed happen if God were only the "Wholly Other." But in

the biblical experience of the encounter, the "Wholly Other" is concerned about man. God's concern for him makes man very real indeed. Religion is not the reduction of man to nothingness, but the elevation of the "nothing" to the reality and responsibility of being, by the attention it receives from the Creator.

15. Psalms 8:5-6.

16. Cf., for instance, Midrash Tehilim 100:3.

17. Psalms 2:11.

18. It is indeed doubtful in what exact sense one may speak of Jewish mysticism. It may be of interest to recall what Gershom Scholem, the contemporary authority on Jewish mysticism, has to say on the sense of separateness among Jewish mystics in his *Major Trends in Jewish Mysticism*: "The fact is that the true and spontaneous feeling of the *merkava* mystic knows nothing of divine immanence; the infinite gulf between the soul and God the King on his throne is not even bridged at the climax of mystical ecstasy... Throughout there remained an almost exaggerated consciousness of God's *otherness*, nor does the identity and individuality of the mystic become blurred even at the height of ecstatic passion." Scholem, *Major Trends*, pp. 55-56. Similarly, Scholem writes that "it is only in extremely rare cases that ecstasy signifies actual union with God, in which the human individuality abandons itself to the rapture of complete submersion in the divine stream. Even in his ecstatic frame of mind, the Jewish mystic almost invariably retains a sense of distance between the Creator and his creature. The latter is joined to the former, and the point where the two meet is of the greatest interest to the mystic, but he does not regard it as constituting anything as extravagant as identity of Creator and creature." Scholem, *Major Trends*, pp. 122-123.

19. Benedict de Spinoza, *The Ethics* 5:36.

20. Cf. Scheler, *Eternal in Man*, p. 196. There is a surprising similarity between Spinoza's *amor dei* and some of the ideas of Thomas Aquinas on the same subject. In Aquinas' *Summa Contra Gentiles* we find such passages as this: "But God wills and loves his essence for its own sake. Now, the divine essence cannot be increased or multiplied in itself... it can be multiplied solely according to its likeness, which is participated by many. God, therefore, wills the multiplicity of

things in willing and loving his own essence and perfection." Aquinas, *Summa Contra Gentiles*, book 1, 75:3.

According to Spinoza, God loves "the multiplicity of things" because they are modes of himself ("God, insofar as he loves himself, loves men..."; Spinoza, *Ethics* 5:36); according to Aquinas, God, insofar as he loves himself, loves the multiplicity of things, for they participate in his likeness. In both cases, God's love is a form of self-love. Aquinas actually maintains that God wills things other than himself because, loving and willing his own being, he desires it to be diffused as much as possible "through the communication of likeness." Cf. Aquinas, *Summa Contra Gentiles*, book 1, 96:3.

About the love of man for God and the love of God for himself, Aquinas writes: "Furthermore, every perfection and goodness found in creatures is proper to God in an essential way... But to love God is the highest perfection of the rational creature... therefore, the love is found in God in an essential way. Therefore, of necessity God loves himself." Aquinas, *Summa Contra Gentiles*, book 1, 80:6. But not only is man's love for God a reflection of God's love for himself; since all perfection and goodness in the "multiplicity of things" are the likeness of the original perfection and goodness which is in God, man's love for God is the effect of God's love for himself. So that we get the Spinozistic conclusion that in man's love for God it is God who loves himself.

Aquinas' position seems to result from his application of the Aristotelian concept of the deity to the biblical framework of Creator and creation. With Aristotle, God can only think himself (cf. chapter two); the Creator, however, must think the world of creation too, think it and will it. How can he do it, if Aristotle is to remain unchallenged? The Thomistic solution is that even in thinking and willing the world, God really thinks and wills only himself. This is what happens when one crosses the Unmoved Mover of the heathens with the biblical idea of the Creator.

Be that as it may, Aquinas' God idea has little in common with that of Isaiah or the Psalms. The God whose throne is the heaven and footstool the earth when he looks "on him that is poor and of a contrite spirit" does not behold his likeness, but that which is the "wholly other" for him, his unlikeness. The Eternal, who is high, "regards the lowly," which is lowly because it is unlike God; he regards man *because* he is lowly. An encounter with oneself is no genuine encounter. God's concern for man is significant because it is directed toward one who is so utterly unlike himself.

21. Our position may be further illustrated by recalling some of the ideas of Friedrich Schleiermacher. According to Schleiermacher, man can in no way respond or react to God. Could man do that, it would be a sign of independence on his part; but an attitude of complete dependence is the religious one. This, of course, means that an encounter between God and man is not really possible. God cannot address man; religion is the obliteration of the human personality. This leads logically to a form of mystical pantheism. And so Schleiermacher sums up his philosophy in the words: "therefore... strive even to annihilate your personality and to live in the One and the All..." Quoted in Hugh R. Mackintosh, *Types of Modern Theology: Schleiermacher to Barth* (London: Nisbet, 1937), p. 55. In our view, however, the sense of complete dependence is a reflection of the objective human situation of "dust and ashes." Religion is the saving of man from this "nothingness." In the encounter with God, man's dependence becomes the source of a measure of independence. Man is granted individuality. He is free to respond to God because God himself protects and respects his gift to man.

CHAPTER FIVE

1. Cf. pp. 15-16.
2. Psalms 16:8.
3. Cf. chapter three.
4. Deuteronomy 29:13-14.
5. The idea has been expressed in many variations in talmudic and midrashic literature. According to Mishna Avot 6:2, "Every day a heavenly voice goes forth from Mount Sinai." Various verses in the Bible are interpreted by the rabbis as enjoining Jews that the Tora

should be for them as if it were given from Sinai "today." Cf., for example, Brachot 63b; see also Yalkut Shimoni on Deuteronomy 26.

6. Psalms 22:2-3.

7. Psalms 22:11-12.

8. Cf. pp. 15-16.

9. Cf. pp. 15-16.

10. About Abraham's "discovery" of God, the mishnaic sage R. Yitzhak says as follows: "The case is like that of the journeyman who saw a palace brilliantly illuminated. Said he: Could it be possible that such a palace should have no master? At that moment, the lord of the palace looked at him and said: I am the master of the palace. Similarly, Abraham asked himself: Could it indeed be that the universe should have no sovereign? And so the Holy One looked at him and said: I am the sovereign of the universe." Genesis Rabba 39:1. It is significant that, according to this midrash, the patriarch started out with the familiar metaphysical questions concerning a Supreme Being as explanation for the existence of the universe. However, it was not his philosophy that led him to God. It was God who showed himself to Abraham in answer to his search. That was the beginning of Judaism. Our point is that those who already know the answer that was granted to Abraham—the descendants of the patriarch who have preserved the family tradition from generation to generation that God "looked at him" and revealed to their ancestor his "leadership" of the world (as the literal text of the midrash has it)—may now, in the possession of such knowledge, turn to the metaphysical quest and rediscover a reflection of the Supreme Being, of which they have learned through the religious experience.

11. Cf. pp. 6-9.

12. Cf. pp. 32-38.

13. Cf. chapter one. Otto, in *Idea of the Holy*, p. 34, makes the point that in religious hymns we find entire chains of negative attributes, which actually say nothing and yet may thrill and intoxicate us. Reading or singing them, we do not notice that the attributes are all negative. He is right, of course; but only for the religious person who knows about God *positively* from the encounter, his own or that

of the founders of his faith. To those, however, who would wish to learn about God from negative attributes, only the logical fallacy of the concept will be communicated.

14. Zephaniah 3:17.

15. Cf. pp. 32-38.

Chapter Six

1. Cf. Maimonides, *Guide of the Perplexed* 1:58.

2. It seems that the translation "I am that I am" (*ehyeh asher ehyeh*; Exodus 3:14) does not do justice to the Hebrew original. The imperfect "*ehyeh*," used here, means continuous being. Cf. E. Kautzsch, ed., *Gesenius' Hebrew Grammar*, trans. Arthur E. Cowley (Oxford: Clarendon, 1910), pp. 334-335. The Hebrew phrase says: "I am continually what I am continually." It expresses the "jutting out" of the divine being into time or—to use some German terminology— the phrase does not speak of *sein* (Being) but of *dasein* (Presence). The correct meaning of the text, therefore, is: I am forever present (for man). The rabbis in the Talmud give it the right interpretation when they remark: "What is the meaning of *ehyeh asher ehyeh*? The Holy One said to Moses: Go and tell Israel that as I have been with them in this subjugation so shall I be with them in their future subjugations by other kingdoms..." Brachot 9b. "I am that I am" is metaphysics, and so was it understood, for instance, by Thomas Aquinas. Cf. his *Summa Contra Gentiles*, book 1, 22:10. The "I am continually present" or "I am forever with them" of the rabbis is religion.

3. Deuteronomy 6:4.

4. Cf. pp. 15-16.

5. Cf. pp. 12-15.

6. Deuteronomy 4:35.

7. The "Alone" of Plotinus fully applies to it.

8. But compare with what has been said above (chapter four) about the "Wholly Other" in relationship to other elements also contained in the encounter.

9. Isaiah 40:12f.

10. Cf. pp. 6-9.

11. It is, therefore, quite possible to hold the most inadequate metaphysical notions concerning God and yet have valid ideas about God's relationship to the world and know about his presence and concern. It is equally possible to penetrate the metaphysical depth of concepts like the Infinite and the Absolute or the All and still have no inkling of the relationship between God and the world. Good religion is not incompatible with poor metaphysics, just as excellent metaphysics by itself in no way provides the basis for a sound religion.

12. The theory was elaborated by Saadia Gaon, Judah Halevi, and Maimonides.

13. Exodus 34:6-7.

14. See Maimonides, *Guide of the Perplexed* 1:54; quoted according to the Chaim Rabin translation, p. 73. Cf. also the comments there by Julius Guttmann.

15. Psalms 103:13.

16. Malachi 3:17.

17. Maimonides, *Guide of the Perplexed* 1:54, p. 74.

CHAPTER SEVEN

1. One will find a penetrating discussion of the conflict between the metaphysical Absolute and the God of religion in Bradley's *Appearance and Reality*, pp. 446-448. While we do not accept either Bradley's interpretation of religion or his solution to this specific problem, we fully subscribe to his statement that "If you identify the Absolute with God, that is not the God of religion. If again you separate them, God becomes a finite factor in the world." We accept this as a valid presentation of the predicament of religious philosphy. Cf. also James Ward, *The Realm of Ends; or, Pluralism and Theism* (Cambridge: Cambridge, 1911), pp. 33f.

2. Ibn Gabirol, in his *Mekor Hayim*, adopts the Neo-Platonic metaphysics and crosses it with the biblical concept of creation. The

Divine will, which Ibn Gabirol interposes between God and a universe in which the various levels of being are connected to each other by emanation, has—of course—no place in Neo-Platonism. The result of Ibn Gabirol's efforts is as barren as are all hybrid products.

3. In Hinduism, too, reality belongs only to the One-All. The world of man is mere shadow and sham.

4. The "negative attributes" are a fine illustration of this intellectual blind alley. To the extent to which they are negative, they represent the Absolute, which has no attributes; insofar as they are attributes, they are positive affirmations about God. Cf. chapter one. The "negative attributes" are, therefore, neither negative nor attributes. What the one term negates, the other affirms, and vice versa. They are as much a contradiction as are the concepts of God and the Absolute. The negative attributes are a symptom of the unresolved conflict between these two.

5. Maimonides did wrestle with this problem, when discussing the question of what could induce the divine Being to create. Cf. Maimonides, *Guide of the Perplexed* 2:14 and 18. We doubt, however, that he fully realized the logical inconsistency of ascribing creation to the Neo-Platonic One, a concept he adopted.

6. Cf. pp. 12-15.

7. This is not the same as saying that God is not only the *causa fiendi* but also the *causa essendi* of the world. (Cf., for example, Maimonides and Descartes.) Even the *causa essendi* explains *how* the cosmos continues to exist. The point we are making is that the most important religious consideration is not *how* the world came to be, nor *how* it continues to be maintained; but *what it is*. The religious idea of creation determines the essence of the universe.

8. Occasionally, the Hebrew equivalent of "creator" is *koneh*, meaning "possessor," and of "creature," *kinyan*, meaning "possession." Cf. Genesis 14:19; Psalms 104:24. See also Mishna Avot 6:10.

9. Cf. chapter four and note 14.

10. Cf. pp. 51-55.

11. Cf. pp. 32-38.

12. Cf. pp. 41-44.

13. Cf. note 11.

14. One encounters the talmudic version of this thought in the interpretation of the meaning of the divine name *shadai*. According to Resh Lakish, the name is a contraction of an entire phrase, which reads, "that—in the act of creation—he called to the world: Enough!" Without that command, the world—as the result of the mightiness of the creative act—might have become limitless. See Hagiga 12a. But since the world did not create itself, God must have given the command to limit the work of creation to himself. We see in this interpretation that the talmudic version of creation is an act of divine self-limitation.

We do not feel competent to judge to what extent our concept of divine self-limitation is identical with R. Isaac Luria's focal concept of *tzimtzum*. If we may go by Gershom Scholem's discussion of the kabbalistic *tzimtzum* in his *Major Trends in Jewish Mysticism*, pp. 260f., it would appear that *tzimtzum* is a withdrawal of divine substance into God in order to make "room" for creation. For us, the act of divine self-limitation is a logical requirement for God's involvement in a finite reality. The important difference seems to lie in the understanding of the act of creation itself. *Tzimtzum* applies to the withdrawal of divine substance in preparation for creation; it is almost a spatial concept. After the withdrawal, God returns to the void in the fullness of his being in order to create. With us, however, self-limitation is not preparatory to creation, but of its very essence. The act of creation demands self-limitation and self-abnegation; otherwise, creation could not be finite. But if it were not finite, it could not be apart from God; in other words, it could not be creation. Furthermore, logically following from *tzimtzum*, the divine attributes are those of divine essence; with us, they are relational attributes, analyzing the divine will in its self-abnegation.

Krochmal's idea of *tzimtzum* need not detain us here. It is the logical outcome of the Hegelian Absolute, which is immanent in the universe. The Absolute may be immanent in the particulars only by shedding its Absoluteness, i.e., by an act of self-limitation. With Krochmal, *tzimtzum* is the logical consequence of a practically pantheistic metaphysics. With Luria, as well as in our discussion, divine self-limitation establishes the reality of the particular and individual, and makes the encounter, and thus religion, possible.

Conclusions similar to these are reached by Ward in *Realm of Ends*, p. 243.

15. Emil Brunner, in his discussion with Karl Barth in *Natural Theology*, trans. John Baillie (London: Centenary Press, 1946), argues that there is no "self-sufficient rational system of natural knowledge of God." We agree with this, but not with Brunner's reasoning. The lack of natural knowledge has nothing to do with the corruptness of human nature, but it is rather the necessary outcome of the finitude of creation. A finite world cannot provide a "natural knowledge" of God, infinite and absolute. Had the first man never sinned, it would not have been otherwise.

16. Psalms 19:2.

17. Psalms 8:4.

CHAPTER EIGHT

1. David Hume, *Enquiry Concerning the Human Understanding*, end of section xi.

2. This is already implied in the words of Saadia, when he says: "All have agreed to accept some view concerning the origin of the world which has no basis in sense perception." Cf. Saadia Gaon, *Book of Doctrines and Beliefs*, p. 51. Saadia, of course, believes that he has found rational proofs for creation. Even if one is unable to follow him there, his point remains valid in the sense that since creation is outside all possible experience, experience can neither prove nor disprove it.

3. Maimonides, *Guide of the Perplexed* 2:17.

4. Maimonides actually removed the idea of creation from the category of causation. Creation is a transcendental concept, outside the realm of all possible experience; causation is a category referring to experience. Many centuries after Maimonides, Kant made a similar distinction. In the *Critique of Pure Reason*, he writes: "And the character of necessity in existence extends no further than the field of

possible experience, and even in this field is not applicable to the existence of things as substances, since substances can never be viewed as empirical effects—that is, as happening and coming to be." That substances are not regarded as empirical effects means that Being itself is not 'caused.' Kant, *Critique of Pure Reason*, p. 248 (B280). For anyone who accepts the idea of creation, this is identical with the insight of Maimonides, who distinguished between causation and creation. See Immanuel Kant, *Critique of Practical Reason* (Indianapolis: Liberal Arts, 1956), pp. 74-110.

5. Actually, while natural selection may explain the elimination of the "unfit," it cannot explain the emergence of the variations from among which it makes its selections.

6. The idea was already clearly expressed in Plato's *Timaeus*. A.E. Taylor, in his *Plato*, has the following to say in the elaboration of Plato's thought: "It is impossible in science to resolve physical reality into a complex of rational laws without a remainder. In the real world there is always, over and above *law*, a factor of the *simply given* or *brute fact*, not accounted for and to be accepted simply as given. It is the business of science never to acquiesce in the merely given, to seek to *explain* it as the consequence, in virtue of rational law, of some simpler initial *given*. But, however far science may carry this procedure, it is always forced to retain some element of brute fact, the merely given, in its account of things. It is the presence in nature of this element of the given, this surd or irrational as it has sometimes been called, which Timaeus appears to be personifying in his language about Necessity." A.E. Taylor, *Plato: The Man and His Work* (London: Methuen, 1929), p. 455.

7. Naturally, the conceiving of the idea itself is not yet the complete act of creation. The creator also develops the form in which his creation is to be executed in the phase of its realization.

8. Obviously, one cannot say that the evolutionary principle is the result of the functioning of the evolutionary principle. One must assume a twofold "givenness" which alone makes evolution possible. The primordial something must be given as well as the evolutionary principle, which causes the evolving of that first "given."

9. Assuming that such a nexus does exist—a point that can no longer be readily admitted in the light of modern scientific inquiry.

10. "Even if the idea of creation be valid, we must necessarily fail to understand the process, just because that cannot fall within our experience; on the other hand any process that we could understand could not be the creative process, because it would fall within our experience." Ward, *Realm of Ends*, p. 245.

11. Genesis 1:31. See Genesis Rabba 9:4, where, in the explanation of this text, we find the following: "R. Hama bar Hanina said: These words may be understood by a simile. A king once had a palace built. He saw it and was pleased. He turned to it with the words: O palace, palace! Would that you please me at all times as you please me at this hour. Similarly, God spoke to the world [after its creation]: O my world, my world! I wish you please me always as you please me now."

See also Genesis Rabba 12:1, where it is said of the works of creation: "Their Creator praises them—who dares defame them? Indeed, they are beautiful and deserving of praise."

Chapter Nine

1. It has rightly been pointed out by Hume that those who derive their proofs for God's existence from the existence of the world are here faced with a hopeless dilemma. Inquiring after the cause of the cosmos, they conclude that there must be a creator. But confronted with the shortcomings in the scheme of creation, they then plead ignorance on grounds that the omnipotent and all-wise God would not have created anything that was not perfect. This argument then leads typically to a vicious circle: Logically, he who knows God from the world has no right to assume any other creator than the one that the world we know justifies. Cf. David Hume, *Dialogues Concerning Natural Religion*, part x.

2. A perfect creation would lead us back to the Neo-Platonic One and to Spinoza's acosmic pantheism.

3. Such a problem, resulting from an implied anthropomorphism, is the old question of Epicurus: "Is he (God) willing to prevent evil, but not able? Then he is impotent. Is he able, but not willing? Then he is malevolent. Is he both able and willing? From where, then, is evil?" Cf. Hume, *Dialogues*, part x; cf. also the discussion by Maimonides, *Guide of the Perplexed* 3:12.

4. Cf. pp. 64-67.

5. Isaiah 45:5-7.

6. According to Neo-Platonism, darkness is only a privation of light. Evil, too, has no reality, and is the result of the absence of the good. Among Jewish philosophers, Saadia accepted this idea. Cf. Saadia Gaon, *Book of Doctrines and Beliefs*, p. 72. Cf. also the note by Alexander Altmann on the same page. See also Saadia's discussion of the passage from Isaiah quoted earlier in this chapter.

7. In composing the traditional morning prayer, the rabbis toned down the boldness of the prophet's phrase by rendering it: "who makes peace and creates *everything*." Cf. Brachot 11b, which shows that they understood the verse as we interpret it. Note also that in accordance with our interpretation of the term, the creation of evil means establishing it as a potentiality.

8. Brachot 60b.

9. In Judaism, Satan is not the mighty angel of rebellion as—in conformity with Christian tradition—he is in Milton. Satan himself is counted among the "sons of God," fulfilling his command and serving him. Cf. Job 1:6. The corollary of Isaiah's concept that God, as the creator of all, "makes peace and creates evil" is the interpretation that the rabbis have offered for the biblical verse: "And you shall love the Eternal your God with all your heart..." (Deuteronomy 6:5) The "all" of the human heart, no less than the universal all, is the abode of good and evil. To love God with all one's heart requires, therefore, loving him with both the inclinations of the heart, the good one as well as the evil. Thus, the evil inclination itself has a function in the service and love of God. Brachot 54a.

10. This argument had already been put forward by the Stoics; see, for example, Windelband, *History of Philosophy*, pp. 195-197. It was

elaborated upon by Bradley in *Appearance and Reality*, pp. 429, 438, 447; also by Ward in *Realm of Ends*, pp. 372-373.

11. The midrash, interpreting the biblical commandment to kindle the Menorah in the sanctuary, gives expression to the thought that God, who is altogether light and in whom there is no darkness, desires the light to be kindled by man because it is light out of darkness. See Midrash Tanhuma, Numbers 8:2.

Chapter Ten

1. See Plato, *Theaetetus* 176a-b and *Laws* 716a-b.
2. Deuteronomy 13:5.
3. Deuteronomy 4:24.
4. Sota 14a.
5. Jeremiah 9:22-23.
6. Leo Baeck points out that in prophetic teaching the knowledge of God means the knowledge and the practice of the good. See Leo Baeck, *The Essence of Judaism* (New York: Schocken, 1948), p. 37. We may explain it by saying: Since God may only be known from the encounter, knowing him implies the knowledge of how to encounter the "other," the world outside ourselves.
7. Several times Kant makes the observation that since the law of practical reason commands us to be better human beings, it follows that we are also able to become better human beings. Cf., for example, Kant, *Religion Within the Limits of Reason Alone*, pp. 15-49; also pp. 55-60. Now this is, of course, unconvincing. It has meaning only on the basis of a dogmatic ontology. That something is required by reason is no proof at all that it is also feasible in practice. On the other hand, it does follow that, if God commands man to become a better human being, the command itself is the assurance that man is, indeed, capable of improvement.
8. Especially since the rise of Christianity, the concept of the law has been exposed to misrepresentation. The difference between Judaism and Christianity is not that the emphasis of Christianity is on the love

of God, whereas in Judaism his stern justice is in the foreground. Whether love or justice, it is always relationship. But a relationship of the Absolute to the finite requires primarily caring involvement—that is, love. The justice of God itself is such a form of caring involvement; its essence is, therefore, love. Divine love may be made manifest in various ways. Thus the Bible says: "And you shall consider in your heart that, as a man chastens his son, so the Eternal your God chastens you." Deuteronomy 8:5. Even the judgment of God, as an expression of his concern, is the proof of his fatherhood. As one of the rabbis in the Talmud expressed it: "Even in the moment of his anger the Holy One remembers his mercy." Pesahim 87b. His very "anger," made possible only by his self-denying act of involvement in the destiny of what is beside him mere "dust and ashes," is a manifestation of his love.

In what specific form divine love ought to be shown depends on our evaluation of man. In the Christian view, as the result of "original sin," man is like a helpless baby. He can exert himself for good as much as he is able to lift himself from the ground by pulling at his bootlaces. For such a creature, a law of God would, indeed, be meaningless. Judaism disagrees with the Christian interpretation of human nature. Man is, of course, not good, but he is capable of goodness. He is a responsible creature. God made his love known to him by entrusting him with a responsibility worthy of his abilities. One does not show one's love to an adult son in the same way as one does in the case of a child. From the Jewish point of view, Christianity has not discovered an idea of God which is superior to the one taught by Judaism; rather, it has adopted a radically pessimistic evaluation of human nature as compared with the critical optimism of Judaism concerning all creation. The Christian God idea is adjusted to the psychological needs of the human being as he is evaluated by Christianity. Cf. Eliezer Berkovits, *Judaism: Fossil or Ferment?* (New York: Philosophical Library, 1956), pp. 53-62.

9. Menahot 43b.

10. A somewhat free translation of the Hebrew *hamuda genuza*. See Shabbat 89a.

11. Psalms 19:8-11.

12. See Rashi's commentary on Genesis 6:9.

13. Cf. R. Joseph Karo, *Shulhan Aruch, Orah Hayim* 2:1-6.

14. Cf. the discussion between the Mutazilites and the Asharites in Islamic theology.

15. Cf. Saadia Gaon, *Book of Doctrines and Beliefs*, pp. 96-97. See also the relevant notes of the editor, Alexander Altmann; cf. also p. 103 and editor's note there.

16. See Windelband, *History of Philosophy*, pp. 332-333.

17. Cf. Kant, *Religion Within the Limits of Reason Alone*, p. 156.

18. In the discussion of this point I owe a great deal to the writings of John MacMurray, especially his *Reason and Emotion* (New York: Barnes and Noble, 1962); as well as to William G. De Burgh's *From Morality to Religion* (London: Macdonald and Evans, 1938). Cf. also Henri Bergson, *The Two Sources of Morality and Religion* (Garden City, N.Y.: Doubleday, 1954).

19. See Plato, *Meno, Protagoras, The Republic,* and *Laws.* Cf. also Taylor, *Plato.*

20. Plato, *Laws* 731c.

21. In Hinduism, for instance, the entire problem would be meaningless. All problems of ethics are problems of individual responsibility. In Hinduism, however, individuality itself is evil. The task, therefore, is not ethical conduct, but conduct in conformity with one's karma, which alone may lead to individual extinction in the All. Cf., for instance, the problem of individual ethical responsibility in the opening verses of the *Bhagavad-Gita* and its solution in the course of the development of the theme of the song.

22. Cf. Taylor, *Plato,* pp. 230, 287; and Plato, *Phaedo* 99c.

23. Our discussion is based, in the main, on the ideas of Julian Huxley as propounded by him in his essays in Thomas H. Huxley and Julian Huxley, *Evolution and Ethics 1893-1943* (London: Pilot, 1947), pp. 106-111. The basic fallacy of all evolutionary ethics is that it is unable to provide the concept of obligation. Evolution describes facts. But what *is* contains nothing that, in itself, may validly propose what *ought* to be. Evolution runs its course in a certain direction, but this

implies no obligation for man to imitate it. Where there is no obligation, there can be no ethics.

24. Cf. Bergson, *Two Sources of Morality*, p. 96.

25. Bergson, *Two Sources of Morality*, p. 101.

26. Bergson, *Two Sources of Morality*, p. 29.

Chapter Eleven

1. We may readily agree with Hobbes that the "will... is the last appetite in deliberating." Thomas Hobbes, *Leviathan* 1:6. We may also readily accept Bertrand Russell's statement that "all systems of ethics embody the desires of those who advocate them." Bertrand Russell, *Religion and Science* (New York: Henry Holt, 1935), p. 242.

2. See note 23 in chapter ten.

3. Cf. pp. 12-16.

4. Maimonides in his *Mishneh Tora*, Laws of Kings 8:11, records the rabbinical teaching that those Gentiles who observe the seven commandments given to "the sons of Noah" are to be considered "the pious of the nations" and have a share in the world to come. However, he adds—and apparently without any support from talmudic sources—that this is true only in cases where the "seven commandments" are observed as the law of God, as revealed in the Bible. It does not, however, apply to those Gentiles who practice them as the result of their grasping of the logical validity of these commandments. It would seem to us that Maimonides' position in this context contradicts the rationalism of his *Guide of the Perplexed*. There, the highest service of God is that of the intellect; here, it seems to be the obeying of a divine command because it is commanded and not because reason "dictates" it.

His position in *Mishneh Tora* seems to imply the point of view presented here. The "seven commandments" have logical validity; but they are laws of God because they were actually commanded by God. Now, a Gentile who practices them because they were revealed by God fulfills the will of God; he is a "pious" man. But he who practices them because he recognizes their logical validity acts in conformity with reason and his own human desire and will. He is, of course, an ethical person; but he cannot be called "pious."

5. Cf. Max Scheler, *Man's Place in Nature* (New York: Noonday, 1961), pp. 63-67.

6. Cf. Berkovits, *Judaism: Fossil or Ferment?* pp. 124-131.

7. In the context of this discussion, we are using the term "matter" in the sense which it has received in modern physics, i.e., as being identical with "energy."

8. Cf. chapters four and seven.

9. Cf. Plato, *Alcibiades I*; see also Taylor, *Plato*, pp. 27-28.

10. See, for example, Aristotle, *On the Soul* 3:9 and 3:10.

11. Aristotle, *On the Soul* 3:9.

12. Cf. Spinoza, *Ethics* 4:14-15.

13. Cf. pp. 81-84.

14. See chapter twelve, note 21.

15. Since we know nothing of God's essence, it is highly doubtful that the "image" of God, in which man was created, could refer to the faculty of reason. The only "image" of God of which we know is reflected in the relational attributes, expressing God's desire for "mercy, justice, and righteousness on earth." To do justice and righteousness and to judge the cause of the poor and the needy is, according to Jeremiah, the meaning of the knowledge of God. Jeremiah 22:15-16; see also chapter ten, note 7. We would rather say that the "good inclination" in man is the "image" of God, in which man was created.

16. In the Talmud, man's natural inclination for the good is compared to a "poor man" who saves the city in his wisdom. See Nedarim 32b.

17. I am not unaware of the importance that the concept of "disinhibiting" has received in modern psychology. No doubt, it is necessary to "disinhibit" the behavior of a person at times, but only in pathological situations. Normally, however, inhibition is the precondition of all civilization and culture.

18. Where no ritually permissible food is available, a man must not endanger his health and is *commanded* to sustain his life with the food he may obtain. See chapter twelve, note 10.

19. On dealing with the "evil inclination" cunningly, see Brachot 5a.

20. We are treating here the significance of the law as a discipline of conduct and its effects on the body. As I suggest further down, this does not exhaust the full meaning of the law. The law does have this habit-forming effect, even though on the level of conscious religious life the rabbis have taught that "a person should not say, 'I do not eat pork because I dislike it.' But rather, 'I do like it; however, what can I do, since the Tora forbade its enjoyment?'" See Sifra Leviticus 20:26.

21. See Jerusalem Brachot 2:10.

22. We have discussed the disciplinary significance of the ritual laws in general. The specific form which these laws were given is, of course, not explained by this discussion. Often it is due to the specific religious purposes which these laws also have, and with which I have dealt in chapter nine. Often, of course, they may depend on historic considerations, like the commandment of eating *matza* on Passover in commemoration of the Exodus. One may even agree that some laws were dictated entirely by certain conditions which prevailed at one time in Jewish history. As is well known, Maimonides explained some ritual laws as having been time-conditioned reactions to certain idolatrous ways of worship and practice. See, for example, his *Guide of the Perplexed* 3:32.

It is not at all illogical to say that some historic necessity determined the specific form of a ritual law. Nevertheless, the law does not pass with the passing of the historic situation. Its specific form might have been time-conditioned; its general significance within the disciplinary system of the law derives from the condition of man. As long as that condition lasts, the law will remain. This applies even more exactly to the general religious significance of the law, about which see further on.

CHAPTER TWELVE

1. Cf. pp. 16-18.

2. Cf. pp. 41-44.

3. Cf. pp. 41-44.

4. There is no need for entering into a discussion of the specific talmudic concept that "*mitzvot* do not require intention" (*mitzvot ein tzrichot kavana*), which may be translated as saying that conscious intention is not a *sine qua non* for adjudging a *mitzva* to have been obeyed.

5. Psalms 35:10.

6. Cf. Maimonides, *Mishneh Tora*, Laws of Prayer 5:9; see also R. Jacob ben Asher, *Arba'a Turim*, *Orah Hayim* 101:2; as well as R. Joseph Karo, *Shulhan Aruch* ad loc.

7. Adapted from Philip Birnbaum's translation in his *Daily Prayer Book* (New York: Hebrew Publishing Company, 1977), p. 334.

8. Kant, *Religion Within the Limits of Reason Alone*, p. 180.

9. Bahya ibn Pakuda differentiated between "duties of the heart" and "duties of the body," but only in order to be able to concentrate all the more on the "duties of the heart." In reality, however, the *mitzva* represents the coalescing of the two categories of duties in the one unifying deed, which should be known as the duty of man.

10. The biblical verse "You shall therefore keep my statutes, and my ordinances, which if a man do, he shall live by them" (Leviticus 18:5) is interpreted by the Talmud to mean that "he shall *live* by them but not that he shall *die* by them." Yoma 85b. On that basis, for instance, whenever the preservation of life conflicts with the observance of the Sabbath, the preservation of life takes precedence. According to the teachings of Judaism, a person must not expose himself to danger needlessly. Cf. Mishna Truma 8:4; Pesahim 112a; Hulin 10a.

11. Cf., for instance, Plato, *Phaedo*.

12. Cf. the blessings that are to be said upon beholding beauty in creation. There are specific blessings which are to be recited when one sees beautiful trees and handsome people. Cf. Brachot 58b.

13. The dining table is compared to the altar in the Temple of Jerusalem. Cf. Karo, *Shulhan Aruch, Orah Hayim* 167:5.

14. The thought comes to clear expression in the Tosefta Brachot 4:5, where we find the following: "R. Meir said:... If a person, on seeing bread, exclaims: Blessed be he who created this bread! How beautiful it is! Then such is its blessing..."

15. See Tosefta Brachot 6:7.

16. See Shabbat 119a, where R. Yehoshua ben Hanania calls the Sabbath the spice that makes the Sabbath dishes savory.

17. Genesis 1:28.

18. Isaiah 45:18.

19. See, for instance, Gitin 41b.

20. Sota 17a.

21. The words of the Bible, "You shall love the Eternal your God with all your heart..." (Deuteronomy 6:5), were interpreted by the rabbis in the Talmud as meaning that a man should love God with everything there is in his heart, that is, with both his inclinations, the good and the evil one. Brachot 54a; cf. also chapter nine, note 9.

22. Cf. pp. 87-90.

23. See Leviticus Rabba 34:3, where Hillel explains to his disciples that the taking of a bath is a *mitzva*, as a deed of respect performed on the body of man.

24. In the history of Western philosophy it was Schiller who, in his *Naive and Sentimental Poetry*, struggled with the problem of man's sensuous nature. We agree with him that the "ethical man" is not the whole man. The "moral state" of man may only be established at the cost of the suppression of his biophysical condition. Had Schiller been familiar with some of the insights of psychology which are available for us now, he might have added that just because of the required suppression, the "moral state" has thus far not been achieved in history. However, it is difficult to accept his solution that by an "esthetic education," which allows the satisfaction of man's sensuous nature "nobly," the two sides of human nature may be reconciled. The ideal is not the "beautiful soul" (*die schone Seele*)—man is not a soul—but body and soul sanctified through the holy deed.

25. The Hebrew *ruah hakodesh* ought not to be translated as "the holy spirit," but rather as "the spirit of holiness." See also Cohen, *Religion of Reason*, ch. vii, pp. 100-112.

26. The Kantian definition of the "true religion" as "the invisible religion of the heart" leads logically to the concept of the "holy will." See Kant, *Critique of Practical Reason*, pp. 30-33, and 20-26.

27. Cf. pp. 102-106.

28. Laws regulating human relationships are stricter than those affecting man's relationship to God. Cf. Sanhedrin 27a.

29. Cf. Mishna Avot 6:2.

30. We use the term which is familiar in the history of religious thought. It should, however, be clear that from our point of view the idea of *mitzvot ma'asiyot* is a tautology. The essence of every *mitzva* is a deed.

31. See the dictum of Rav in Genesis Rabba 44:1.

Chapter Thirteen

1. See Eliezer Berkovits, "The Galut of Judaism," *Judaism* 4:3 (Summer 1955), pp. 225-234, where I have argued that any attempt at interpreting Israel as a purely religious association of believers is a distortion, not only of the historic concept of Israel, but also of the ideological contents of Judaism.

2. The result of "idealistic" religions and philosophies, usually sadly ineffective and often guilt-laden in history, has prompted a great deal of partisan nonsense concerning the tribal and national religion of the Jews. Cf. Eliezer Berkovits, *Judaism: Fossil or Ferment?* pp. 33-82.

3. Cf. R. Travers Herford's discussion of the overwhelming importance of the creed in Christianity. See his *The Pharisees* (New York: Macmillan, 1924). Heresy hunting is the typical affliction of all "idealistic" religions. In Judaism, in contrast, wrong opinions are not punishable, only wrong deeds.

4. In *Religion Within the Limits of Reason Alone*, Kant has the following to say on the effectiveness of the ideal of the good: "The

highest moral good cannot be achieved merely by the exertions of the single individual toward his own moral perfection, but requires rather a union of such individuals into a whole toward the same goal—into a system of well-disposed men in which and through whose unity alone the highest moral good can come to pass..." Kant, *Religion Within the Limits of Reason Alone*, p. 89.

5. Genesis 12:1.

6. Exodus 19:6.

7. On Jewish universalism, cf. Berkovits, *Judaism: Fossil or Ferment?* pp. 62-75.

8. See the traditional prayer *Aleinu.*

9. Jeremiah 2:3.

10. Cf. earlier in our discussion, pp. 100-104.

CHAPTER FOURTEEN

1. Psalms 44:23.

2. Even before the birth of the Jewish people, it was announced to the patriarch Abraham: "Know well that your offspring shall be strangers in a land not theirs..." Genesis 15:13.

3. Cf. the main theme of the book of Job; see also Habakkuk 1:13 and Brachot 7a.

4. Cf. pp. 106-110.

5. See, for example, Windelband, *History of Philosophy*, pp. 195-197, regarding the discussion of the problem by the Stoics. See also the discussion of the same subject in the little volume by Sallustius, translated by Gilbert Murray and published by him as an appendix to his *Five Stages of Greek Religion* (Boston: Beacon, 1935).

6. A characteristic saying of R. Hama bar Hanina is that "everything is in the power of heaven, except the fear of heaven." Brachot 33b.

7. Kant could not accept the idea that an ethical law should have to emanate from the will of the Supreme Being. He believed that such a law could not be considered ethical but rather compulsory and legalistic, nor would the resulting fulfillment of duty be an expression of "free virtue." Cf. Kant, *Religion Within the Limits of Reason Alone*,

pp. 90–91. Kant was right in insisting that freedom cannot be separated from ethical action. Any action performed under duress cannot be ethical. At the same time, an ethical principle must be obligatory, and obligation derives from a commanding will. Kant assumed that only "the moral feeling" and "practical reason" may provide an ethical law in freedom. The truth is, as we have shown, that they allow too much freedom and thus reduce ethics to complete subjectivity. For us, the will of God is the source of the absolute objectivity of the ethical law. The necessary element of freedom is safeguarded by the "hiding" of God. While the desire of God constitutes the law, it is conveyed to man in such a manner that most of the time, man is free to refuse to acknowledge the manifestation of God's will.

8. Zephaniah 3:17.

9. About such indirect intervention in order to punish an evildoer who cannot be brought to justice, cf., for instance, Makot 10b; Sanhedrin 37b; Ketubot 30b.

10. See Hume, *Enquiry Concerning the Human Understanding*, sec. x, note 21.

11. Benedict de Spinoza, *A Theologico-Political Treatise*, trans. R.E. Elwes (New York: Dover, 1951), p. 92.

12. Spinoza, *Theologico-Political Treatise*, p. 83.

13. Cf. pp. 15–16.

14. Cf. pp. 78–81.

15. It is, indeed, not impossible to interpret the "laws" of nature as nature's God-granted independence from the Creator. Through the laws, God might have put his creation on its feet, as it were, enabling it to go its own way (to some extent). Without such laws, all creation would be in continuous danger of disintegration because of its perpetual chaos, and God would have the task of continually re-creating the cosmos. All order would be due to the direct intervention of God; all would be miracle and utter dependence. "God created," however, means that he posited something outside himself; he gave his creation an identity of its own; he let it be itself. Even nature can be itself only if it possesses its identity with some measure of freedom. The laws of nature, for all we know, may be a manifestation of such identity; they may be an indication of the course that nature

chose for itself. Since God protects and preserves man's identity in moral freedom and responsibility, why could not the relationship between God and his entire creation be a similar one? To outside observation the laws may appear as a chain of necessity, speaking still in terms of classical physics; looked at from "within," however, they may be expressions of nature's impulses, urges, and desires in the midst of limited areas of "freedom" and "choice." Nature itself may possess some spontaneity and be capable of doing right or wrong. Whatever freedom and independence there might be within nature would have to be limited by divine responsibility for the act of creation. While God, in granting a separate identity to the world, took a risk with his works, the risk would nevertheless have to be a calculated one. As human freedom may often result in man-caused suffering, so may nature's freedom at times lead to nature-caused suffering of the innocent and pure. And as in history, so, too, in nature may the Creator's ultimate responsibility occasionally require divine intervention.

16. Zechariah 14:9.

17. Zephaniah 3:17.

18. Cf., for example, Shabbat 119b.

19. According to the midrash, "The gates are always open, and everyone who wishes to enter may do so." Exodus Rabba 19:4.

20. It is noteworthy that the teachers of the midrash applied the words of Ecclesiastes, "that which is crooked cannot be made straight," only to the world to come, in which one reaps the rewards of one's conduct in the present world. But as long as man lives on earth, the crooked may well be made straight, for none of his actions are final. There is always the possibility of Return. See Ecclesiastes Rabba 1:15.

21. Sanhedrin 97b. Cf. Yoma 86b; Maimonides, *Mishneh Tora*, Laws of Repentance 7:5.

22. See Pirkei d'Rabi Eliezer 43.

23. See Eruvin 13b.

24. This should not be confused with Kant's postulate of immortality. All of Kant's postulates derive from requirements of "practical reason." Since the human soul is never able to achieve the highest good in time, there must be a timeless existence in which the soul

may achieve it, which is immortality. Similarly, since bliss (*gluckseligkeit*) is a form of harmony between the moral state of man and the state of physical nature, there must be a cause external to nature that implants the possibility of such harmony in advance. This cause is the Supreme Being. These postulates are subject to all the criticism that is rightly leveled against every form of ontology. "Practical reason" demands that the soul be able to acquire the highest good, but this does not justify the expectation that the soul will ever acquire it; the possibility of *gluckseligkeit* requires the positing of a Supreme Being as the originator of moral and physical nature, but this need not mean that such a Being does exist; it may be that *gluckseligkeit* is not to be achieved. The postulates that we employ emanate not from a principle of reason, but from the reality of God's existence. The existence of God and the nature of his relationship to man and the world being given, the postulate of immortality follows of necessity.

Index